AF618985

VIRON EROL VERT

THE NAME OF SHADES OF PARANOIA, CALLED DIFFERENT FORMS OF SILENCE

AUSSTELLUNGSKATALOG EXHIBITION CATALOGUE

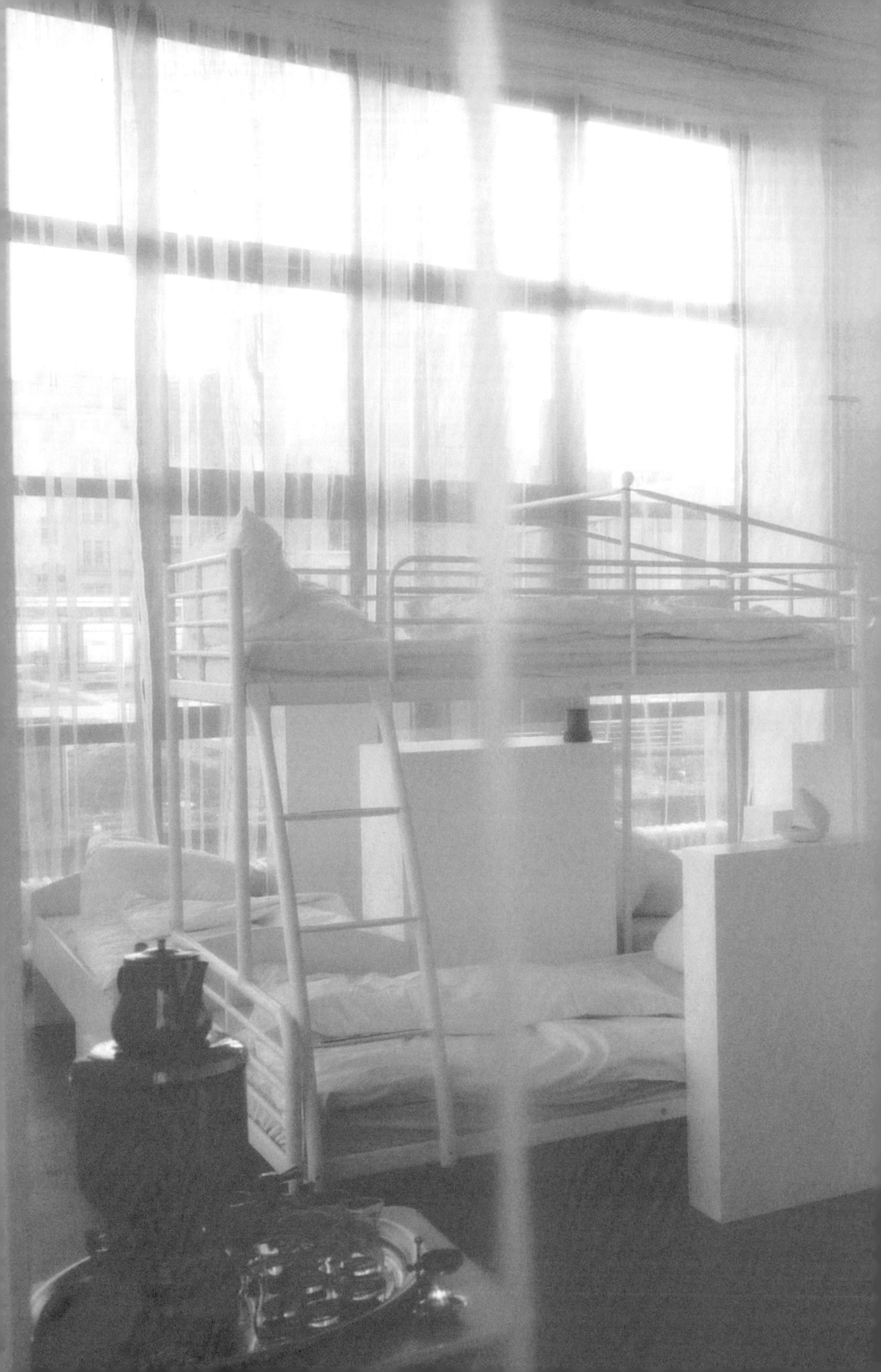

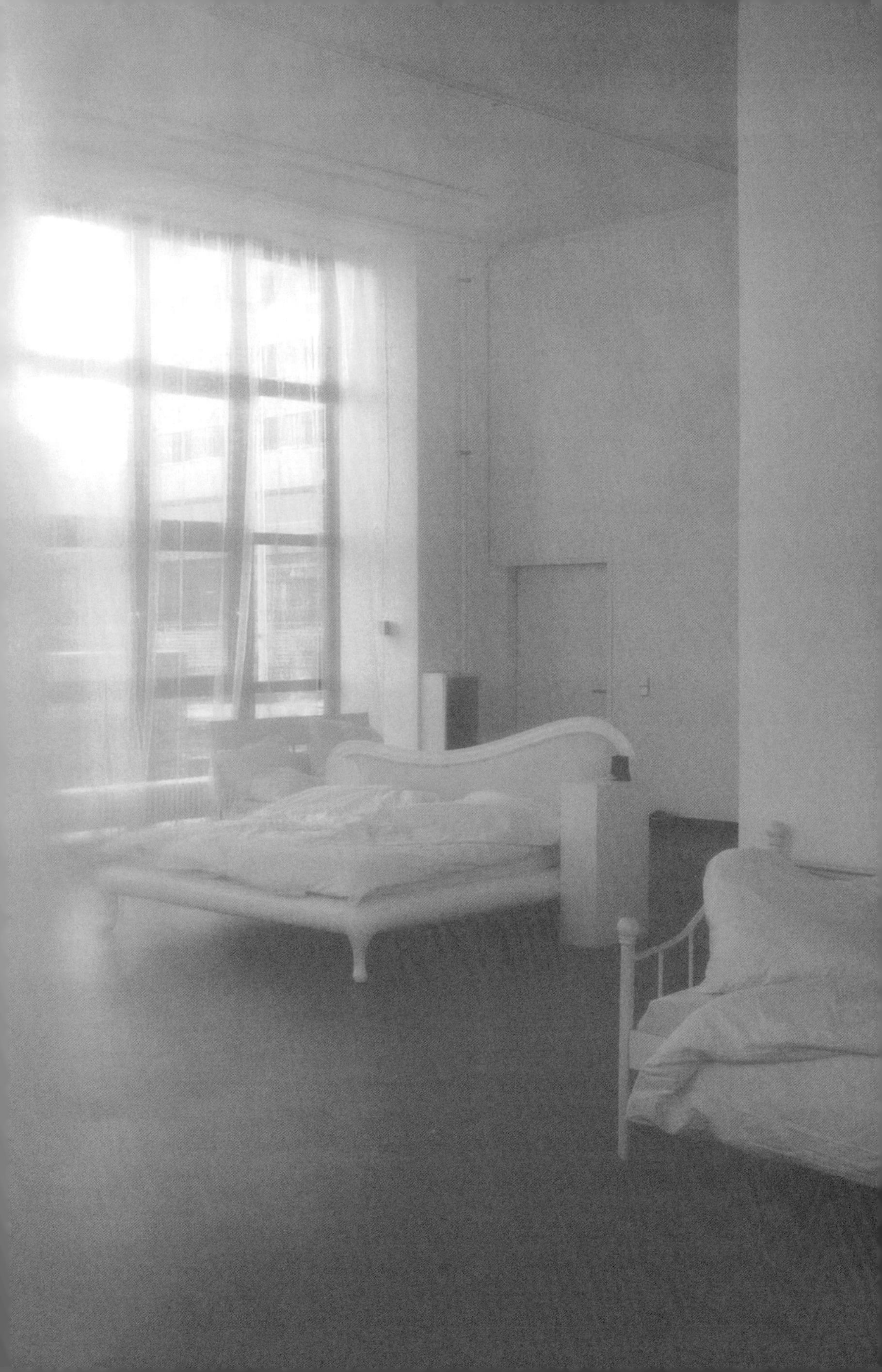

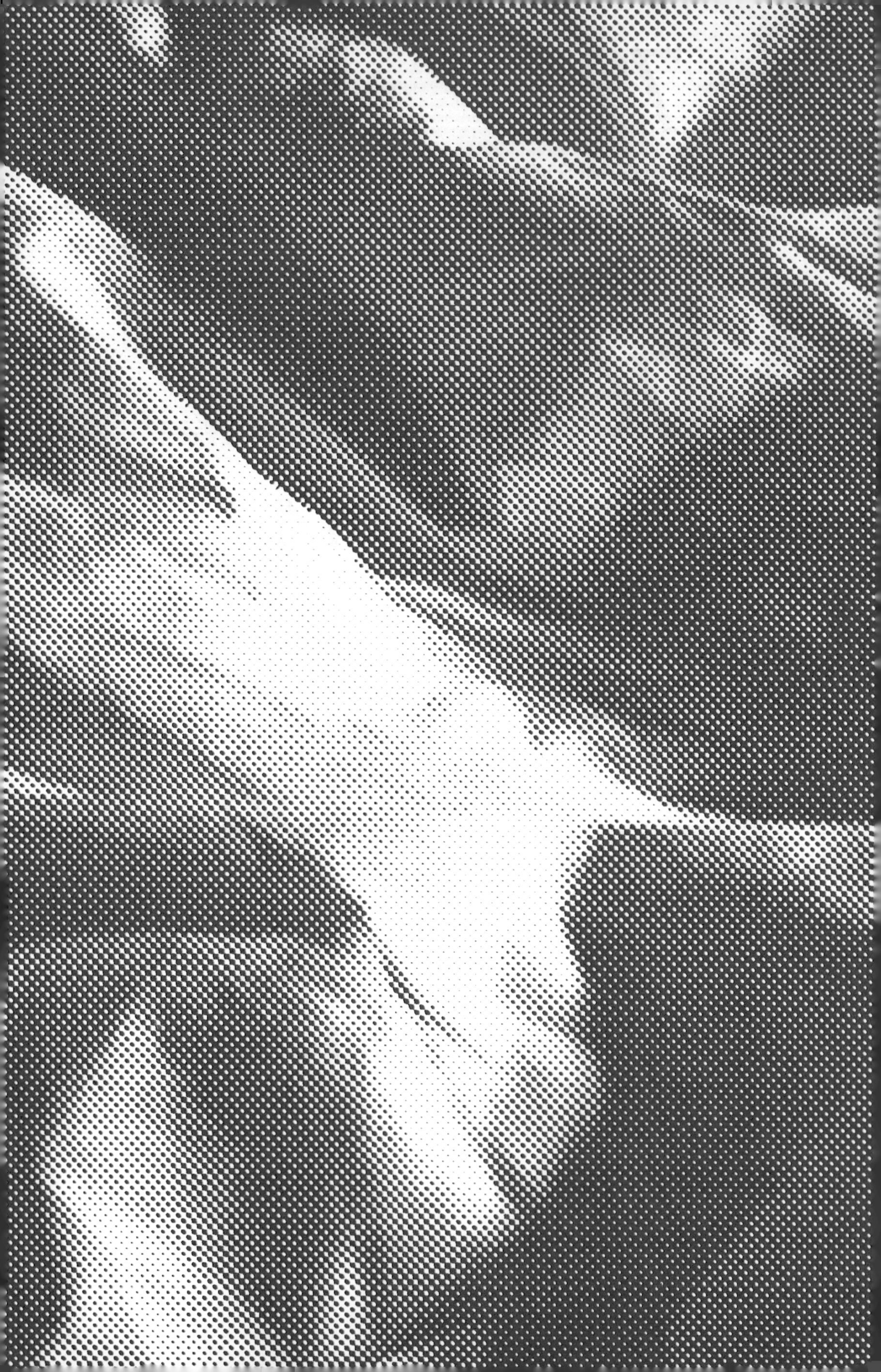

Ute Müller-Tischler

VORWORT

INTRODUCTION

DE

Aus der Kulturgeschichte der Antike und des Mittelalters wissen wir, dass seit jeher Traumvisionen eine große Bedeutung zugemessen wurde. Seit Jahrtausenden zeichnen Menschen Träume auf, um ihr Leben und ihre Zukunft zu deuten. In künstlerischen und literarischen Überlieferungen tauchen quer über den Globus Bilder von Traumsequenzen und Traumtechniken auf. In Traumhandbüchern des mittelalterlichen, islamischen Kulturkreises spielen sie eine bemerkenswert wichtige Rolle, auch im jüdisch und christlich geprägten Europa werden Erinnerungen an Träume kulturell ritualisiert. Als wiederkehrende Narrative beeinflussen sie bis heute den mythologischen, spirituellen Gehalt vieler Kunstwerke. Spätestens mit der Moderne jedoch wird versucht, die Wunder des Träumens in die Welt der wirklichen Gegenwart zu holen.

EN

We know from the cultural history of antiquity and the Middle Ages that great significance has long been attributed to dream visions. For millennia, people have been recording dreams to gain insight into their lives and future. Images of dream sequences and dreaming techniques are found in the artistic and literary traditions of cultures from all around the world. They play a remarkably important role in dream handbooks from the medieval Islamic cultural sphere, but recollections of dreams were also culturally ritualised in Judaeo-Christian Europe. As recurring narratives, they still influence the mythological and spiritual content of many artworks today. Furthermore, at least since the modern period, attempts have been made to bring the miracle of dreaming into the real, present world. Numerous scientific analyses have

Zahlreiche wissenschaftliche Untersuchungen entstehen, allen voran die psychoanalytische Traumdeutung, mit der uns Sigmund Freud bahnbrechende Grundlagen für die Kunst des 20. Jahrhunderts liefert und damit ganze Generationen beeinflusst. Und noch immer liegt dem Unbewussten unserer Traumzustände ein verborgenes Geheimnis zugrunde. Die Sehnsucht danach, die flüchtigen Bilder des Schlafes zu enträtseln, inspiriert Künste wie Neurowissenschaften der Gegenwart nach wie vor gleichermaßen und erlebt gerade wieder Aufmerksamkeit.

Der deutsch-türkische Künstler Viron Erol Vert baute mit seiner Ausstellung »The Name of Shades of Paranoia, Called Different Forms of Silence« in der Galerie Wedding ein »Dreamatory« – eine Art Traumlabor. Hinter den hohen Glasfronten verwandelte er mit halbtransparenten Stoffbahnen den sonst durchlässigen Ausstellungsraum an der Müllerstraße in einen Rückzugsort für Gestresste und Gefährdete. Alle, die sich hier aufhielten, konnten sich in der weißen Bettenlandschaft seiner Raumintervention in den Zustand tiefer Entspanntheit versetzen,

been developed: the psychoanalytic interpretation of dreams led the way and was utilised by Sigmund Freud to provide us with innovative new foundations for the art of the twentieth century, thus influencing entire generations. Nonetheless, the unconscious of our dreaming state still remains founded on a hidden mystery. The yearning to decipher the fleeting images of sleep continues to inspire the arts and neurosciences of the present as much as ever and is receiving renewed attention at the moment.

In his exhibition »The Name of Shades of Paranoia, Called Different Forms of Silence«, the Turkish-German artist Viron Erol Vert built a »Dreamatory« – a kind of dream laboratory – in the Galerie Wedding. He used lengths of semi-transparent cloth behind the gallery's floor-to-ceiling front windows to transform this otherwise open exhibition space on Müllerstraße into a place of refuge for those suffering from stress and vulnerability. All of the visitors who spent time in the white »bedscape« of his art intervention could place themselves in a state of deep relaxation, follow

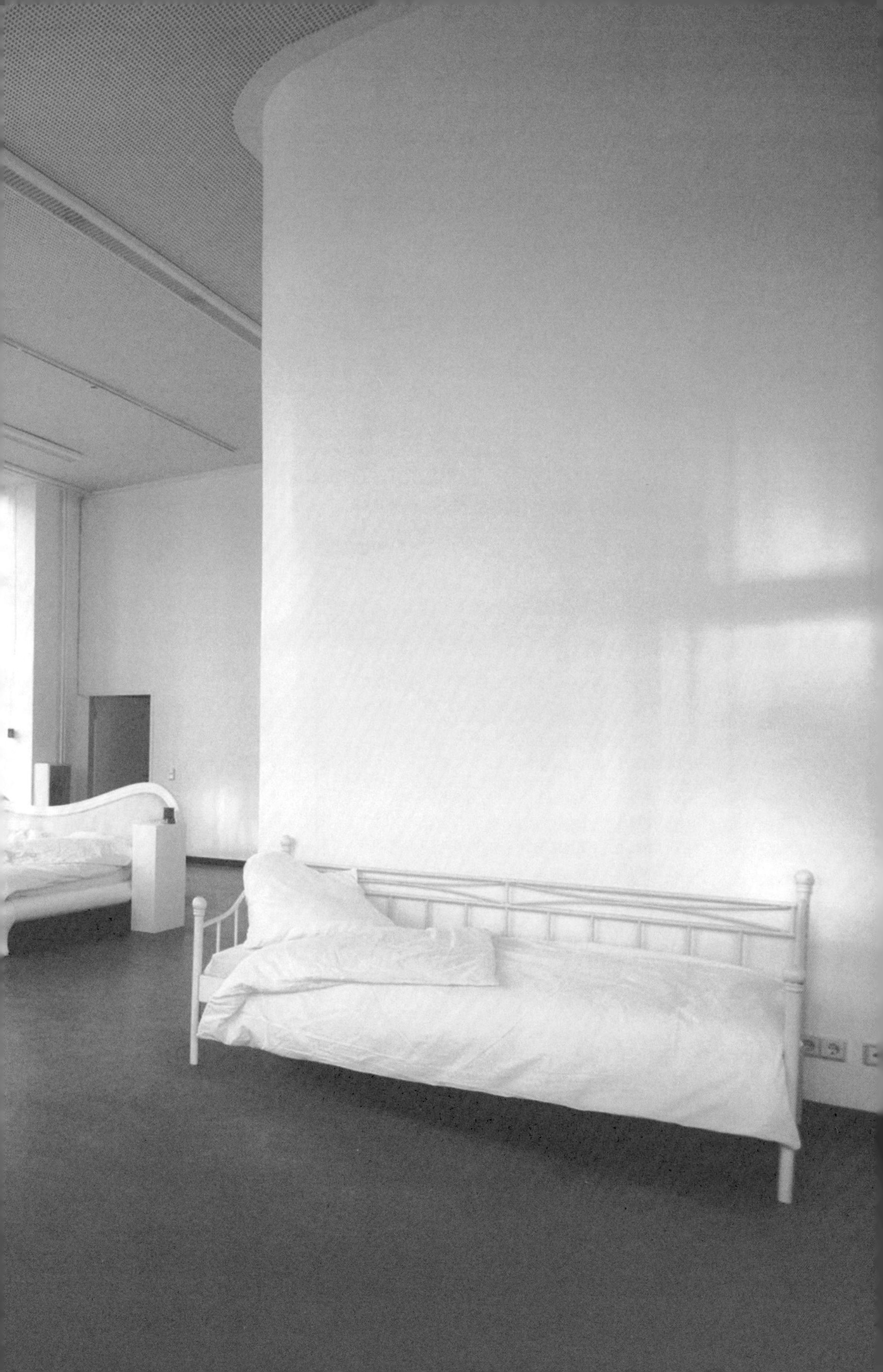

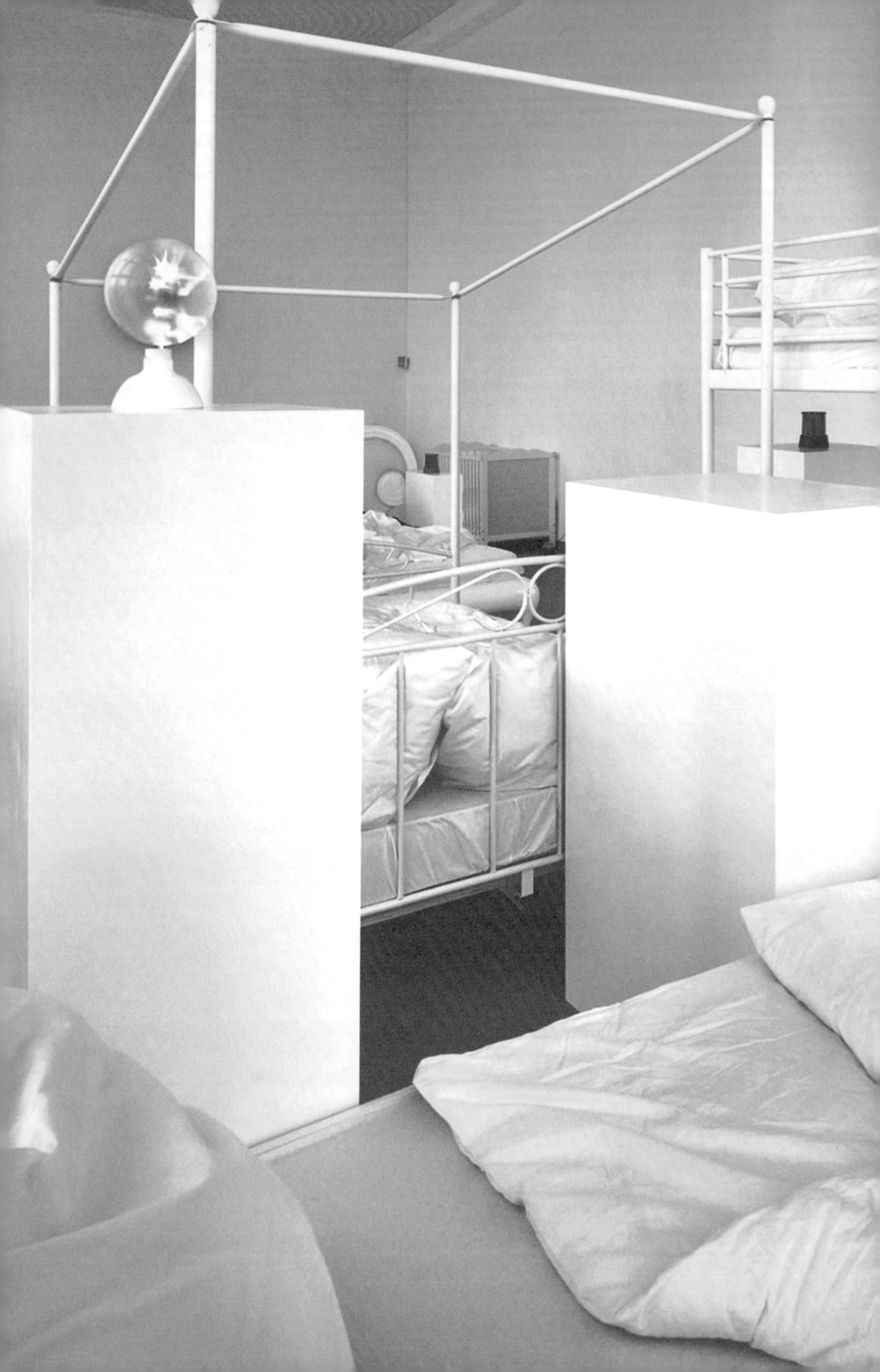

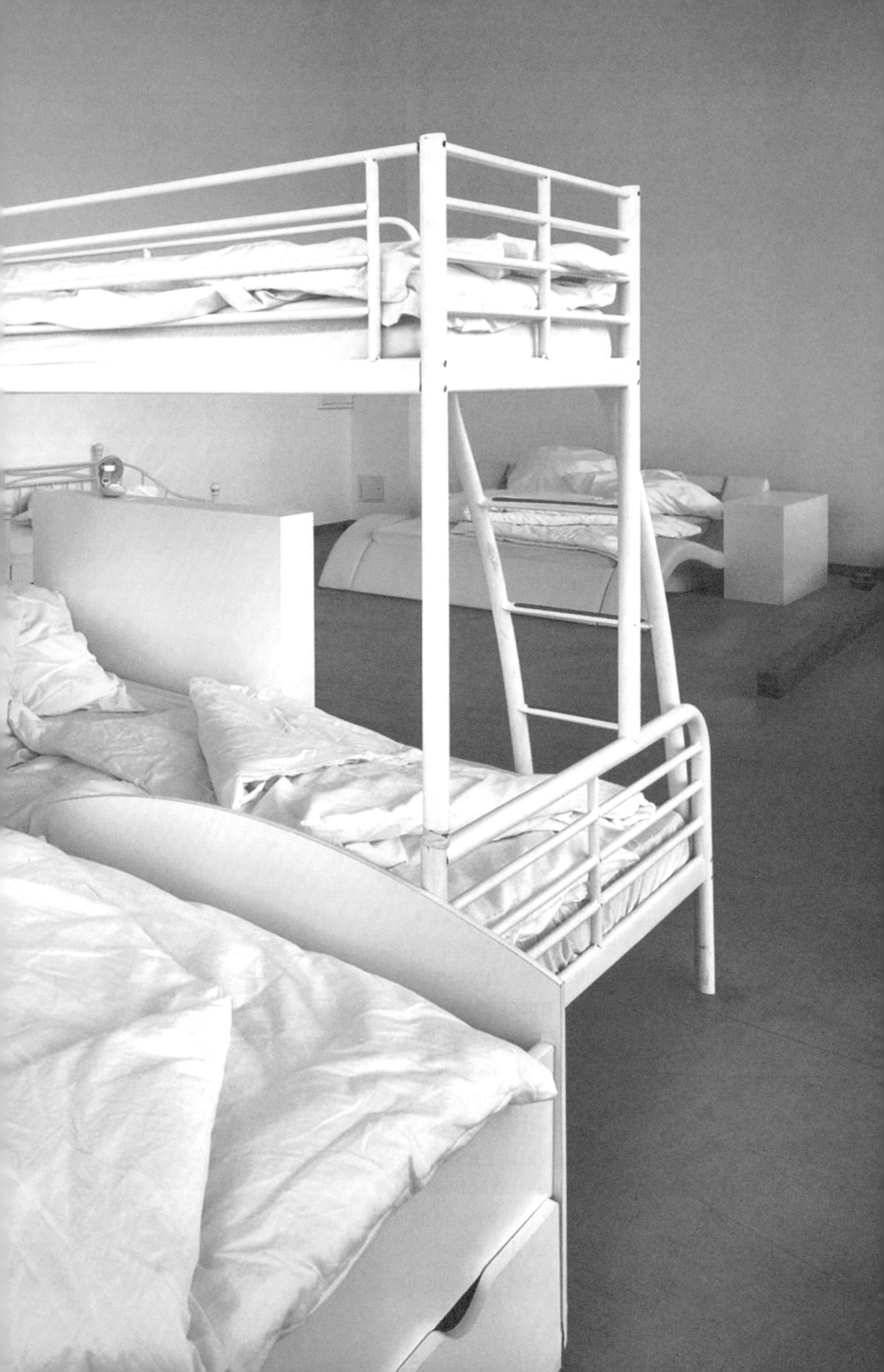

ihren Gedanken wie im Traum nachgehen und sie wie den Verkehr vor den Fenstern vorüberziehen lassen. »In diesen Augenblicken empfinde ich die Neu-Verbindung zu unseren inneren Welten, unseren Träumen und Ängsten«, formuliert Viron Erol Vert sein Anliegen in diesem Dokumentationsband. Phantasie und Träume können seiner Ansicht nach helfen, die Vorkommnisse unserer Zeit aus anderen Blickwinkeln zu analysieren und auf diese Weise veraltete Konzepte und statische Strukturen aufzulösen. So wie die Surrealist*innen Träume als zentrale Inspirationsquelle für ihre künstlerischen Verfahren nutzten, wollte er mit der Raumanordnung seiner Installation die Mechanismen des rationalen Denkens außer Kraft setzen und den Blick nach innen lenken. Angesichts weltweiter Sprachlosigkeit und politischer Ratlosigkeit gegenüber den chaotischen Zuständen unserer Zeit möchte er die verschiedenen Mythologien und Traditionen aus der Vergangenheit mit heutigen ästhetischen Wertvorstellungen kollidieren lassen. Einen Krieg der Träume zu entfachen, hieße, im Aufprall wesensfremder Elemente unsere unbewussten und rätselhaf-

the train of their thoughts as though in a dream and let them flow past like the traffic outside the windows. »In these moments, I sense a reconnection with our inner worlds, our dreams and fears«, is how Vert expresses his goal in this volume documenting the project. He believes that fantasy and dreams can help us to analyse the events of our time from other perspectives and, in this way, break up outdated concepts and static structures. Just as the Surrealists utilised dreams as a central source of inspiration for their artistic processes, he wanted to use the arranged space of his installation to suspend the mechanisms of rational thought and direct our gaze inward. In the face of worldwide speechlessness and political perplexity regarding the chaotic conditions of our time, he would like to cause the various mythologies and traditions of the past to collide with current notions of aesthetic ideals. Unleashing a war of dreams would mean using the collision of incommensurable elements to uncover our unconscious and enigmatic worlds and discover unimagined answers in them.

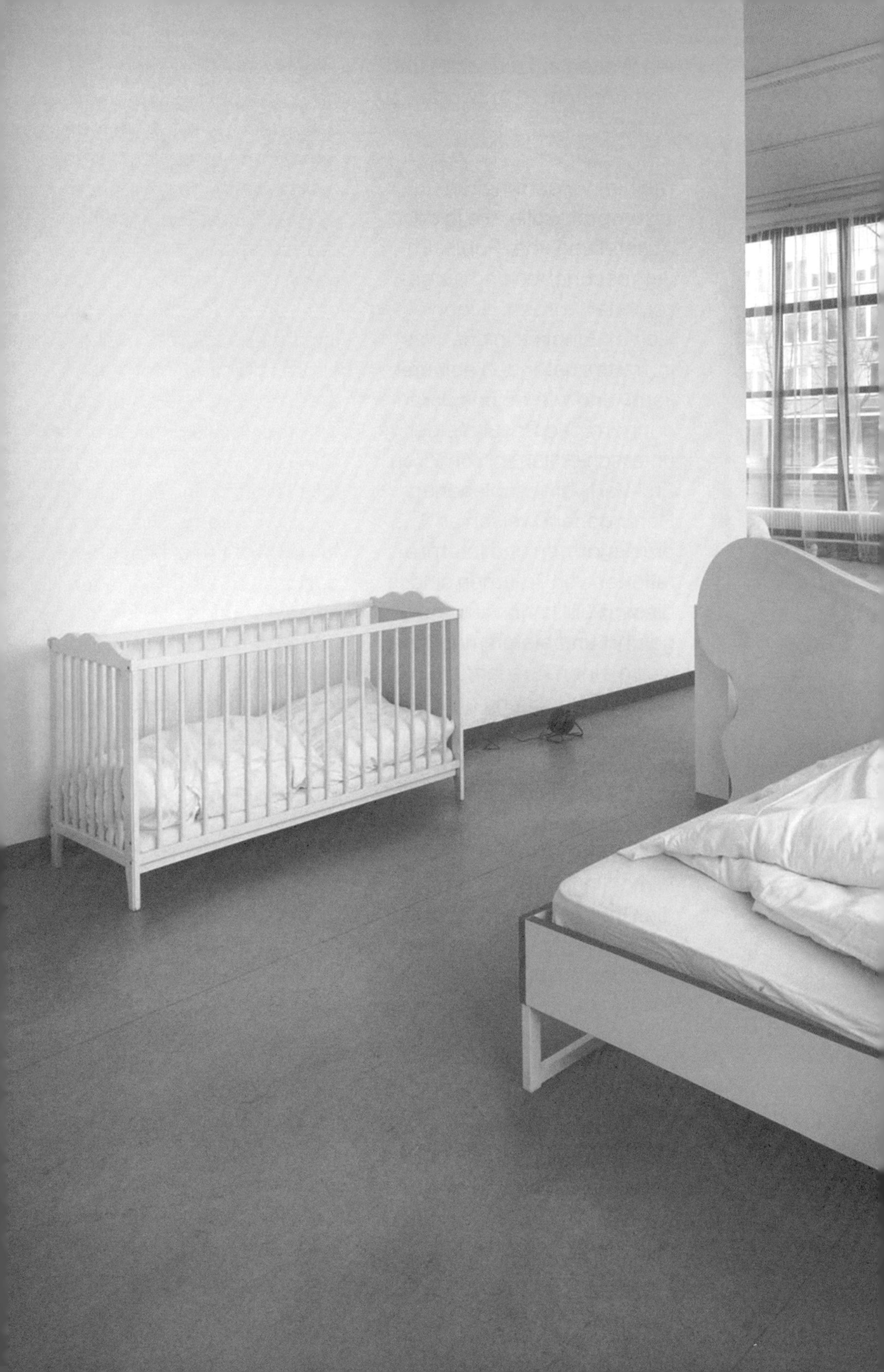

ten Welten aufzudecken und dort ungeahnte Antworten zu finden.

Die hier versammelten Traumprotokolle, die in der Ausstellung vom Publikum aufgeschrieben und aufgezeichnet wurden, geben einen kleinen Einblick in das, was in Traumzuständen ablaufen kann, und wie wir uns daran erinnern. Die Resultate der unterschiedlichen, von Viron Erol Vert vorgeschlagenen Herangehensweisen an Ausdrucksformen und Interpretationen von Träumen sind in dieser Publikation zusammengeführt und bieten möglicherweise einen Ausgangspunkt für die Erforschung und Darstellung der eigenen Träume. In Bild und Text werden neben den Ausstellungsansichten und Performances wunderbare Beiträge wie Yusuf Etimans Filmcollage »Kino Morph« und die Oneiroi-critics-Session mit dem Psychotherapeuten Michael Mollura aus Beverly Hills dokumentiert.

Die Galerie Wedding dankt allen, die bei der Entstehung dieses Ausstellungsprojektes und des vorliegenden Büchleins zur Seite standen und wertvolle Beiträge beigesteuert haben. An erster Stelle bedanken wir uns bei Viron

The dream-diary material gathered here – written or recorded by visitors to the exhibition – provides a small glimpse into the sequences of events that can unfold in dreaming states and how we remember them. The results of Vert's suggestions regarding various approaches to expressing and interpreting dreams have been brought together in this publication and may offer a point of departure for exploring and representing our own dreams. In addition to views of the exhibition and performances, the wonderful contributions of Yusuf Etiman's film collage »Kino Morph« and the Oneiroi critics session with Beverly Hills psychoanalyst Michael Mollura are documented through images and text.

The Galerie Wedding thanks everyone who stood by us and provided valuable contributions during the development of this exhibition project and the present book. First of all we extend our thanks to Viron Erol Vert for this inspiring exhibition and his assistance in sorting through and selecting the documents to be published. We would particularly like to thank those who took part in the dream congress »Talk_about_Dreams – At

Erol Vert für diese inspirierende Ausstellung und für seine Mitarbeit bei der Sichtung und Auswahl der zu veröffentlichenden Dokumente. Bedanken möchten wir uns besonders bei den Teilnehmer*innen des Traumkongresses »Talk_about_Dreams—At the Edge of Consciousness. Sightseeing in the Realm of Dreams«, den Elena Agudio und Joerg Fingerhut vom Institut »Association of Neuroesthetics« (AoN) im Rahmen der Ausstellung organisiert haben. Ohne die wissenschaftlichen Beiträge aus den unterschiedlichen Bereichen der Schlaf- und Traumforschung wäre die multiperspektivische Sicht auf das Thema nicht möglich gewesen. Herzlichen Dank deshalb an Amna Ghani vom Fach Computational Neuro-science an der Charité – Universitätsmedizin Berlin, an Holger Brohm, der »Kulturen des Traumes« im Fachbereich der Kulturwissenschaftlichen Ästhetik am Institut für Kulturwissenschaft der Humboldt-Universität zu Berlin lehrt, und an den Mediziner Pascal Grosse, dem Leiter der Neurologischen Schlafmedizin der Klinik für Neurologie mit Experimenteller Neurologie in der Universitätsklinik Charité.

the Edge of Consciousness: Sightseeing in the Realm of Dreams« , which was organised by the neuroscientist Elena Agudio and Joerg Fingerhut from the institute »Association of Neuroesthetics« (AoN) to accompany the exhibition. Without the scientific contributions from the different fields of sleep and dream research, our multi-perspectival look at the theme would not have been possible. We thus extend our warm gratitude to Amna Ghani, from the field of Computational Neuroscience at the Charité – Universitätsmedizin Berlin; Holger Brohm, who teaches »Kulturen des Traumes« (Cultures of the dream) in the programme for Kulturwissenschaftliche Ästhetik (Cultural history and theory of aesthetics) at the Humboldt-Universität of Berlin's Department of Cultural History and Theory; and medical doctor Pascal Grosse, head of neurological sleep medicine at the Universitätsklinik Charité's clinic for experimental medicine.

Last but not least, we thank the Berlin graphic art and design office Form und Konzept, whose savvy shaped this volume; the musicians

Und last but not least bedanken wir uns beim Berliner Grafik- und Designbüro Form und Konzept, das den Band klug gestaltet hat, bei den Musikern von »Driftmachine«, deren Soundkonzept der »Oneiro-Triologie« dafür die Struktur lieferte, bei den Lektor*innen und Übersetzer*innen und selbstverständlich bei Marie-Christin Lender und Nadia Pilchowski, deren umsichtige Arbeit bei der Redaktion des Buches und Zusammenarbeit mit dem Verlag wichtig für dessen Gelingen war.

Vor allem den beiden Kurator*innen der Ausstellung, Solvej Helweg Ovesen und Bonaventure Soh Ndikung, sei zum Schluss gedankt, deren Programm UP (Unsustainable Privileges) Themen der Migration für den Kunstkontext aufgreift und so unaufdringlich wie unmissverständlich immer wieder nach einer neuen Verteilung von Privilegien, auch der unserer Träume, fragt. Ihr Blick in die Kulturgesellschaft unserer Zeit und ihrer beunruhigenden Konfliktzonen hat den Reflexionsraum der Galerie erweitert und zu einem zeitgenössischen Ort der Stadt Berlin gemacht.

Ich wünsche viel Vergnügen bei der Lektüre.

of Driftmachine, whose audio concept for their Oneiro-Trilogie provided it with its structure; our copy editors and translators; and of course Marie-Christin Lender and Nadia Pilchowski, whose conscientious efforts in editing this book and working with our publisher were important for its successful completion.

Finally, and above all, we would like to thank the exhibition's two curators, Solvej Helweg Ovesen and Bonaventure Soh Ndikung, whose UP (Unsustainable Privileges) programme introduces migration-related themes into an art context and is no less subtle than unequivocal in repeatedly asking questions about a redistribution of privileges – including those of our dreams. Their insight into the cultural society of our time and its unsettling conflict zones has expanded the reflective space of the gallery and made it a key contemporary location in the city of Berlin.

I hope you enjoy reading this book!

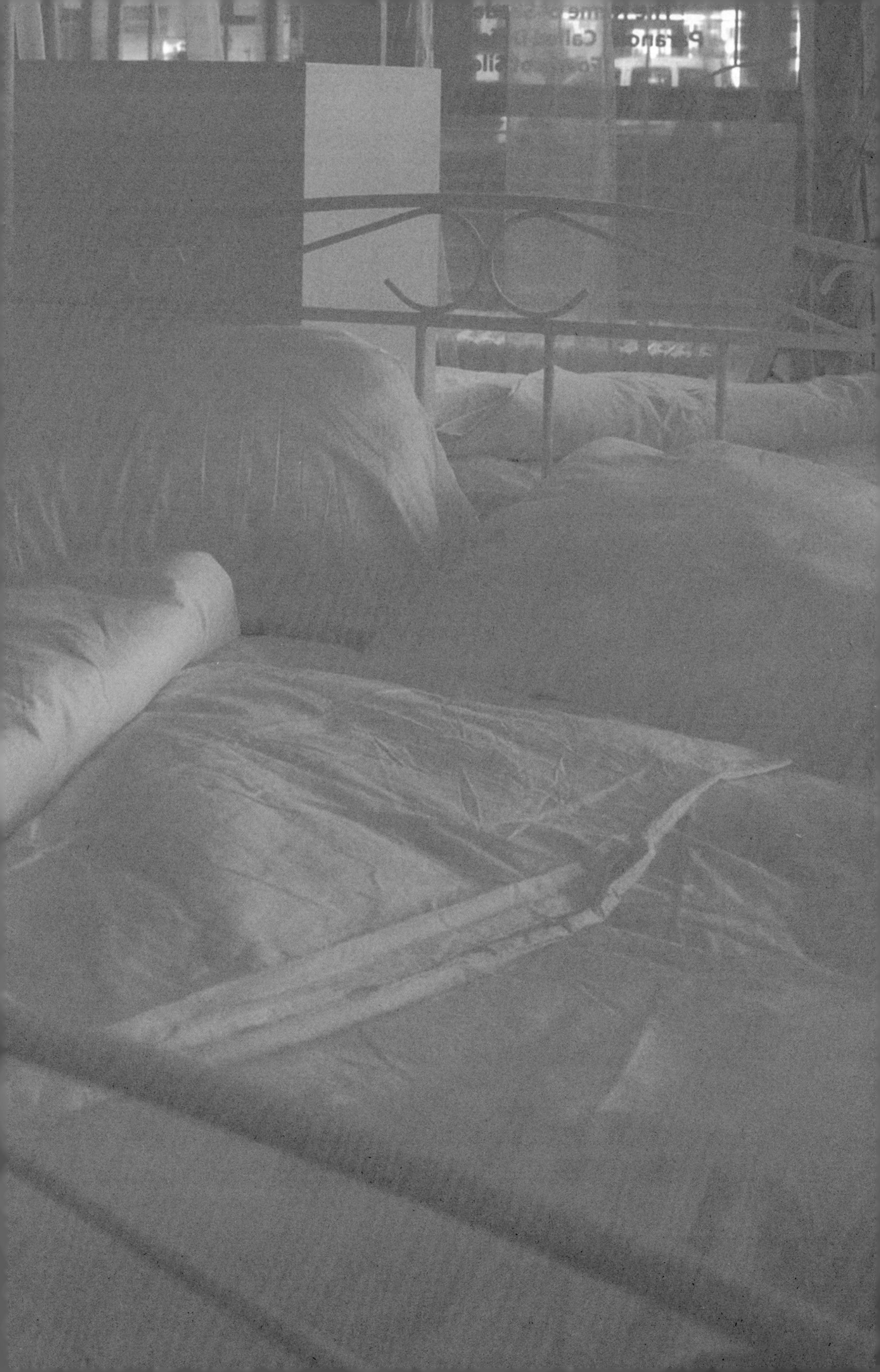

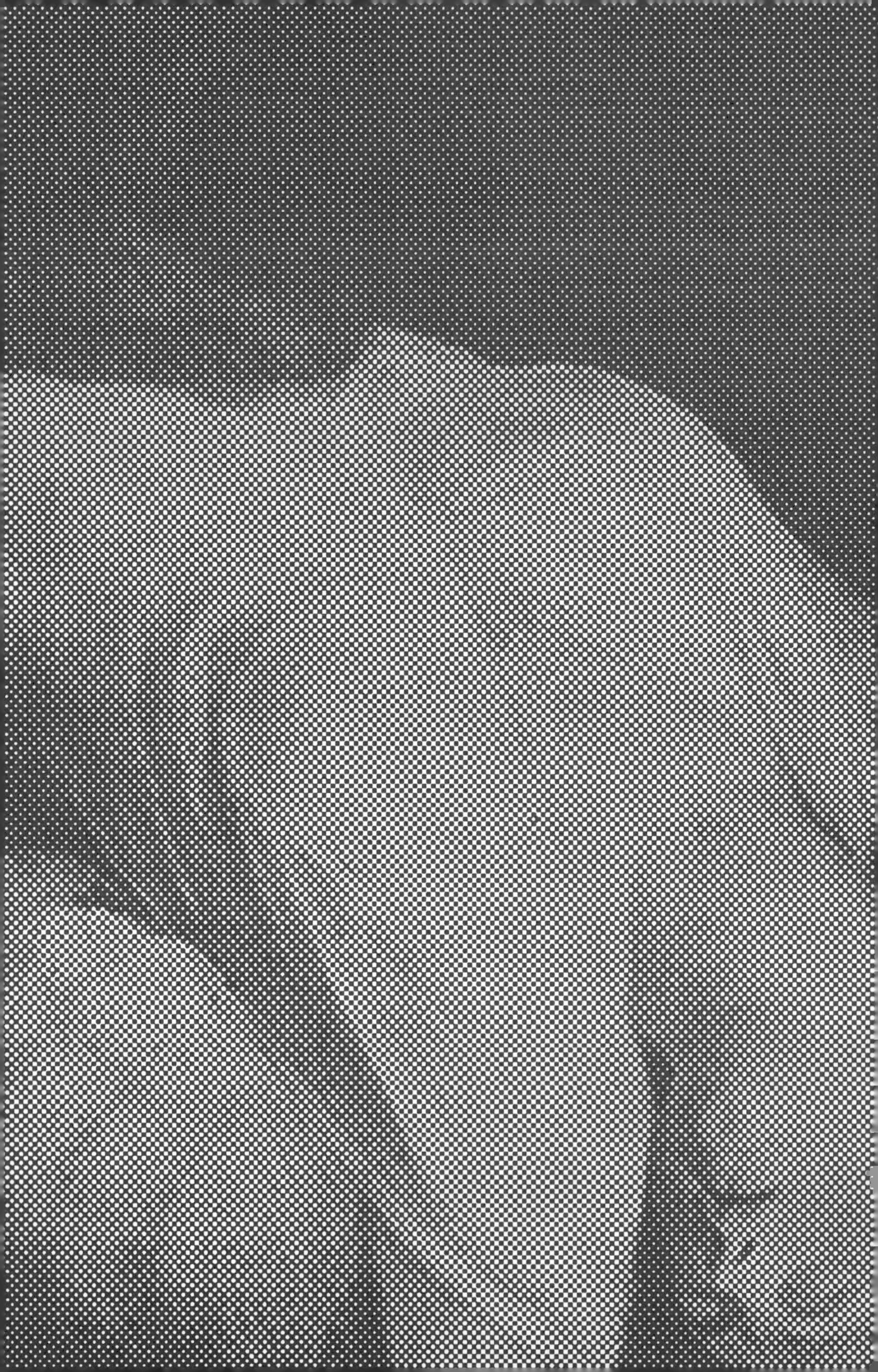

Bonaventure Soh Bejeng Ndikung

»THE NAME OF SHADES OF PARANOIA, CALLED DIFFERENT FORMS OF SILENCE« EIN DREAMATORY-VORHABEN

»THE NAME OF SHADES OF PARANOIA, CALLED DIFFERENT FORMS OF SILENCE« A DREAMATORY PROPOSITION

DE

In dem brillanten kurzen Essay »Istanbul was our past, Istanbul is our future«[1] (Istanbul war unsere Vergangenheit, Istanbul ist unsere Zukunft), veröffentlicht nach den schrecklichen und unerträglichen Angriffen in Istanbul in der Silvesternacht 2016/17, stellt der stets zum Nachdenken anregende Hamid Dabashi eine Reihe von essenziellen Fragen, Fragen, die nach solchen maßlos grausamen Taten uns alle beschäftigen. Er fragt, worauf diese Dummheit abzielt, wogegen sie sich richtet, welche Art von Gefühlen sie wohl auf solch primitive Art und Weise auslösen will. Dabashi zufolge ist der Angriff auf einen Club an diesem symbolischen Tag ein Angriff auf die Kultur der Toleranz, auf den tatsächli-

EN

In his brilliant short essay »Istanbul was our past, Istanbul is our future«,[1] published after the horrific and unbearable attacks in Istanbul on New Year's Eve 2016/17, the ever thought provoking Hamid Dabashi poses a set of rather crucial questions, which are indeed questions gyrating in everyone's mind after such acts of proportionless savagery. He asked: »What is this inanity targeting? What is it, that it is opposing? What kind of sentiment, however crudely, does it want to provoke?« And according to Dabashi, the reason for the attack of a nightclub on that symbolic day is thus an attack »on the culture of tolerance, on the factual pluralism of Muslim countries now in many ways represented in Istanbul.«

1 Hamid Dabashi, Istanbul was our past, Istanbul is our future, 2017, available via www.aljazeera.com/indepth/opinion/2017/01/istanbul-istanbul-future-170103074202409.html (retrieved 10.01.2017).

chen Pluralismus muslimischer Länder, der heutzutage in vielerlei Hinsicht in Istanbul vertreten ist.

Nach jeder derartigen Tat, ob verübt durch ISIL, Boko Haram, al-Shabab, al-Qaida, durch einen einsamen Verrückten oder wen auch immer, sei es in Kaduna, Bagdad, Jakarta, Paris, London oder Berlin – die Tendenz geht immer dahin, sie als Taten gegen eine Kultur der Toleranz zu sehen und zu verhandeln. Während Dabashi überzeugend argumentiert, dass Muslimen und Nicht-Muslimen innerhalb und außerhalb der islamischen Welt ein grausames Gefecht bevorstehe, nicht bezogen auf Identität, aber auf Alterität – es gehe nicht darum, wer sie sind, sondern wer ihr Erzfeind ist –, halte ich es für sinnvoll, eine alternative Ursache zu suchen oder zumindest über eine mögliche Motivation für solche Attentate nachzudenken: Angst.

Es ist gut möglich, dass Angst heutzutage die mächtigste Währung ist, und die blühende Wirtschaft der Angst mag der einfache Kausalzusammenhang von solchen Taten sein. Dies ist aber bei Weitem nicht auf offene

After every such act, be it by ISIL, Boko Haram, Al Shabab, Al Qaida, some lonesome lunatic or what-/whoever might be the perpetrators, and be it in Kaduna, Baghdad, Jakarta, Paris, London or Berlin, the tendency is to look at them and treat them as acts against a culture of tolerance. While Dabashi later makes a strong point that »Muslims and non-Muslims, in and out of Islamic world, are facing a vicious battle, not of identity, but of alterity – not who they are, but who their nemesis is«, I think it worthwhile proposing an alternative reason, or at least speculating on a possible incentive behind such attacks. Fear.

Today, fear might have become the most puissant currency, and a thriving economy of fear might be the simple cause-effect of such acts. But surely this is in no way limited to such overt and loud acts of violence. Fear is a weapon used by sovereignties from Cameroon through China, USA, Turkey to Brazil, as a means to pluck the feathers of civilians, so that they fly below and ordinary pitch. It is fear that is the catalyst used to mobilise thousands of people to go on the streets like Pegida does, in order to

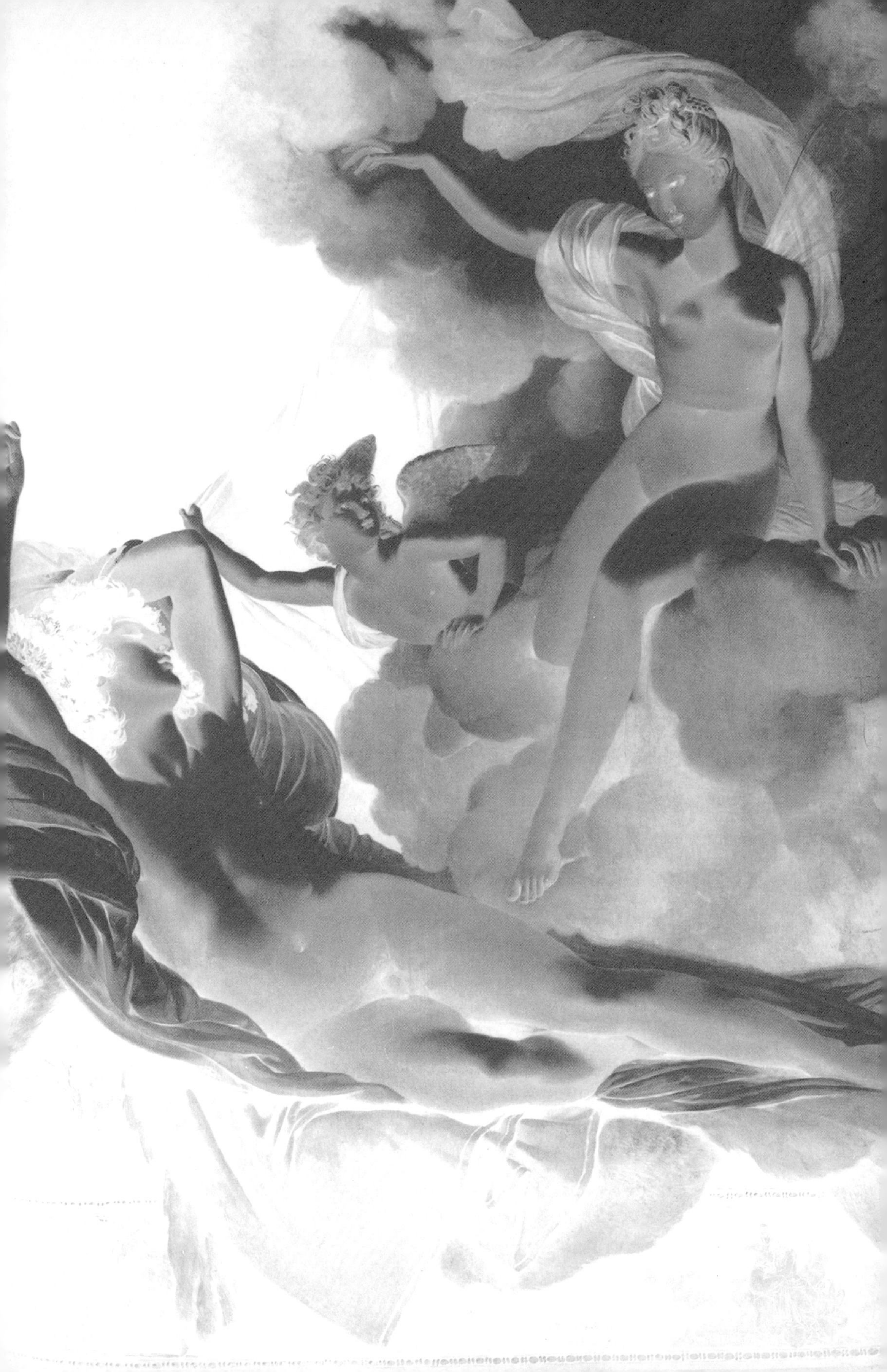

und lautstarke Gewalttaten beschränkt. Angst ist eine Waffe, die von Staatshoheiten von Kamerun über China, die USA und die Türkei bis nach Brasilien benutzt wird, sie ist ein Mittel, um der Zivilbevölkerung die Federn zu rupfen, so dass sie tiefer und in unauffälliger Höhe fliegt. Es ist Angst, die benutzt wird, um tausende Menschen auf den Straßen zu mobilisieren, wie es Pegida tut, um gegen Fremde zu protestieren, die nach Deutschland kommen und angeblich Deutschen die Jobs oder die Frauen wegnehmen. Es ist Angst, die der Gemeinschaft eingejagt werden soll, wenn solche Ansammlungen sich in der Öffentlichkeit präsentieren. Es ist Angst, welche die AfD zur Welt gebracht hat und sie nährt. Es ist auch Angst, auf der Trump einerseits seine Kampagne aufbaute und die andererseits der Nährboden ist, auf dem seine Regierung wachsen und gedeihen wird.

Angst ist die Währung, mit der man Hass kauft. Angst ist das Zahlungsmittel für den Erwerb von Paranoia – jenen mentalen Zustand des Misstrauens, des Argwohns, des Verfolgungswahns, der unbegründeten Eifersucht oder der übertriebenen

protest against that fabrication of the foreigner who comes into Germany to take away German jobs and even German women. It is fear that is meant to be imposed on the community when such a mass presents itself in the public. It is fear that has birthed and breeds the AfD. It is fear too on which Trump built his campaign and fear too is the substrate on which his government will grow and thrive.

Fear is the currency with which hate is bought. Fear is the legal tender for the acquisition of paranoia – that mental state of mistrust, suspicion, delusions of persecution, unwarranted jealousy, or exaggerated self-importance, which is the blues and rhythm of our era. For fear is a two-headed snake. Once it has eliminated and silenced all others around it, it battles itself so as to be the lonesome spitter of venom. But as for now, in these times of dire existential and sociopolitical crisis, in these times when democracy seems to be in a cul-de-sac, and neoliberal capitalist economy is the order of the day, the ubiquitousness of fear paralyses societies and its ferocious »Drang« for destruction and suppression can only

Selbstgefälligkeit, die der »rhythm and blues« unseres Zeitalters sind. Denn Angst ist eine Schlange. Sobald sie alle anderen um sich herum versammelt und zum Schweigen gebracht hat, kämpft sie mit sich selbst, um letztendlich die Einzige zu sein. In Zeiten fataler existenzieller und soziopolitischer Krisen, in Zeiten, in denen die Demokratie in einer Sackgasse zu stecken scheint und die neoliberale kapitalistische Ökonomie auf der Tagesordnung steht, paralysiert die Allgegenwärtigkeit von Angst Gesellschaften, und ihr grausamer Drang nach Zerstörung und Unterdrückung kann nur beschwichtigt werden, indem Gesellschaften und Individuen gelähmt und zum Schweigen gebracht werden. In Michel-Rolph Trouillots Worten: Angst züchtet das Zum-Schweigen-Bringen der Gegenwart.[2] Und es ist dieses Zum-Schweigen-Bringen der Mehrheit, das in der Vergangenheit zu noch größeren Gräueltaten in der Welt geführt hat.

Wir leben aber, wie James Baldwin 1970 in einem offenen Brief an Angela Davis[3] schrieb, in einem Zeitalter, in dem Schweigen nicht nur kriminell, sondern lebensmüde

be pacified when societies and individuals are lamed and silenced. To twist and twerk on Michel-Rolph Trouillot, fear breeds the silencing of the present.[2] And it is the silencing of the majority that has led to even bigger atrocities in the world in the past.

The world we are building is a world of steel,
glass and wind swept mines.
Tomorrow's world is no longer virginal,
but ravaged and open to all
like some unrestrained slut.
The dreams we chase are dreams of shining platinum.
The world we walk is a world of poverty.
The situation that imprisons us is the gaping jaw of a jackal.

Our fate flies like a cloud
opposing and mocking us,
becoming mist in the sleep of night
and sun in the work we do each day.
We will die in the riddle of our fate
with arrogant and clenched hands.
Hands that rebel and labor.
Hands that tear at the sacred envelope
and unfold the holy letter
written in difficult characters we cannot read.

Rendra (Willibrordus Surendra Broto Rendra), »Testimony«, 1967

2 Michel-Rolph Trouillot, Silencing the Past: Power and the Production of History, Boston 1997.

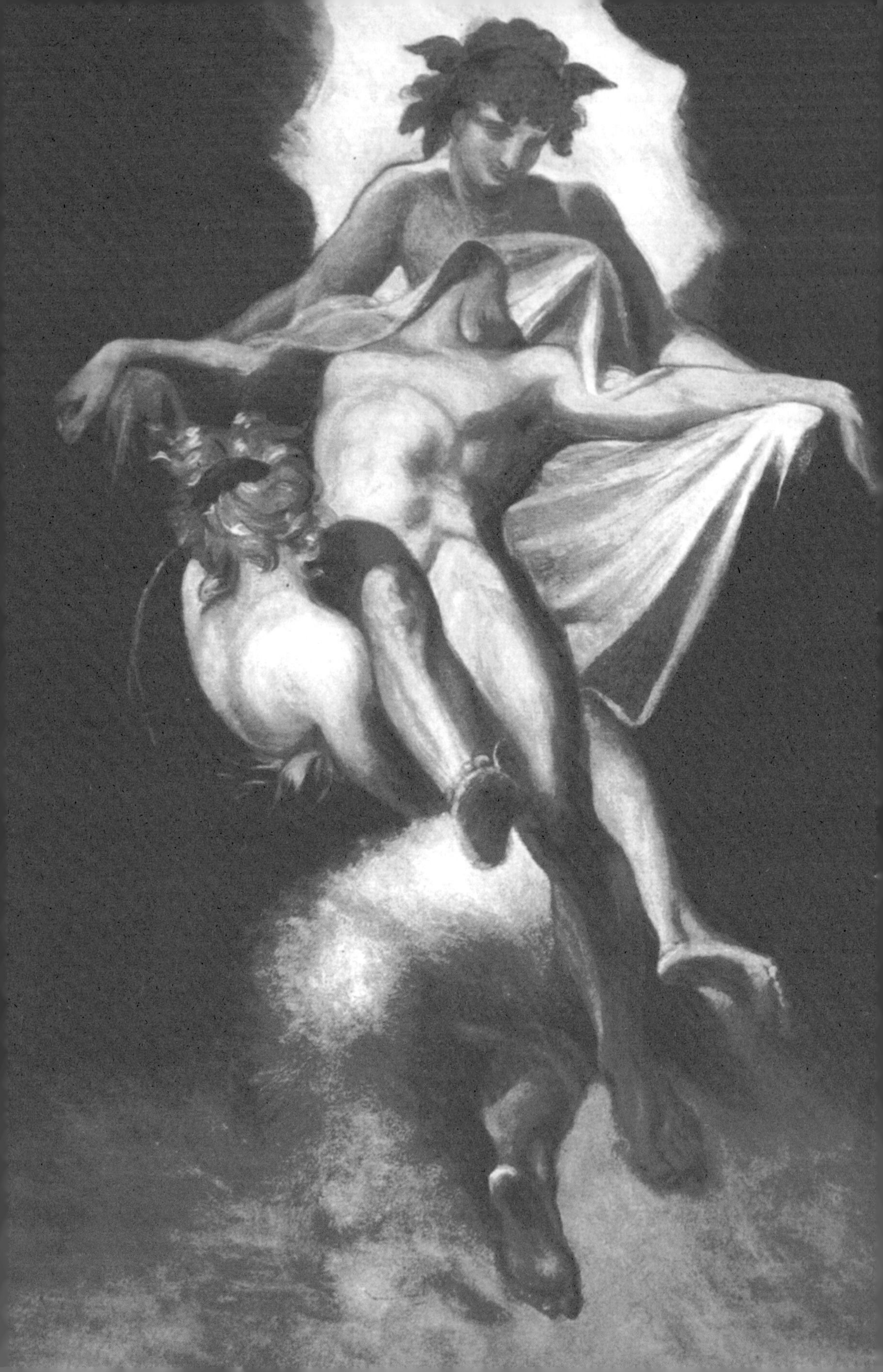

ist. Deswegen nahm er sich das Recht und sah sich in der Pflicht, seine Stimme zu erheben, um auf die erbärmlichen Verhältnisse aufmerksam zu machen, die viele Menschen ertragen müssen. Tatsächlich ist das Schweigen kein Ausdruck von Neutralität, da es tatsächlich bedeutet, Partei für den Unterdrücker und den Aggressor zu ergreifen. Paranoia ist ein Zustand der Lähmung, der Neutralisierung, der Gefühllosigkeit. Aber was soll man machen, wenn die Folgen der Äußerung, des Brechens des Schweigens zu so etwas führen, was im Januar 2017 mit Şansal oder 2007 mit Dink geschah? Was soll man machen, wenn Menschenleben aufs Spiel gesetzt werden, sobald die diktatorische Herrschaft des Schweigens gebrochen wird? Was macht man, wenn man nicht an der Ökonomie und Politik von Risikobereitschaft, Märtyrerspielen und Heldenkomplexen teilhaben will? An dieser Stelle kommt Kunst, d.h. Poesie ins Spiel. Kunst und ihre poetischen Anordnungen können der Raum von Reflexion und Ausdruck sein. Das ist ein Vorschlag, den Viron Erol Vert macht.

But as James Baldwin wrote in his open letter to Angela Davis in 1970,[3] we live in an age in which silence is not only criminal but suicidal, and that is why he took upon himself the right and duty to speak out and make noise about the deplorable conditions some have to face. Indeed, silence is not a position of neutrality, as it actually means taking the side of the oppressor and aggressor. Paranoia as a state of lameness, of neutralisation, of numbness. Which is a weapon of power too, to keep people silent. That is the case Baldwin was making. A case to wake up from that paranoia and numbness.

But what to do when the repercussions of utterance, of breaking the silence lead to what happened to Şansal in January 2017 or Dink in 2007? But what to do when life is at stake if the dictatorial reign of silence is fractured? What to do if one doesn't want to get into the economy and politics of risk-taking, playing the martyr, or the hero-complex? It is at this juncture that art, i.e. poetry comes into play. Art and its poetic dispositions can be that space of reflection and of expression. This is one proposition that Viron Erol Vert is making.

3 James Baldwin, An Open Letter to My Sister, Miss Angela Davis, 1971, available via http://www.nybooks.com/articles/1971/01/07/an-open-letter-to-my-sister-miss-angela-davis/ (retrieved 10.01.2017).

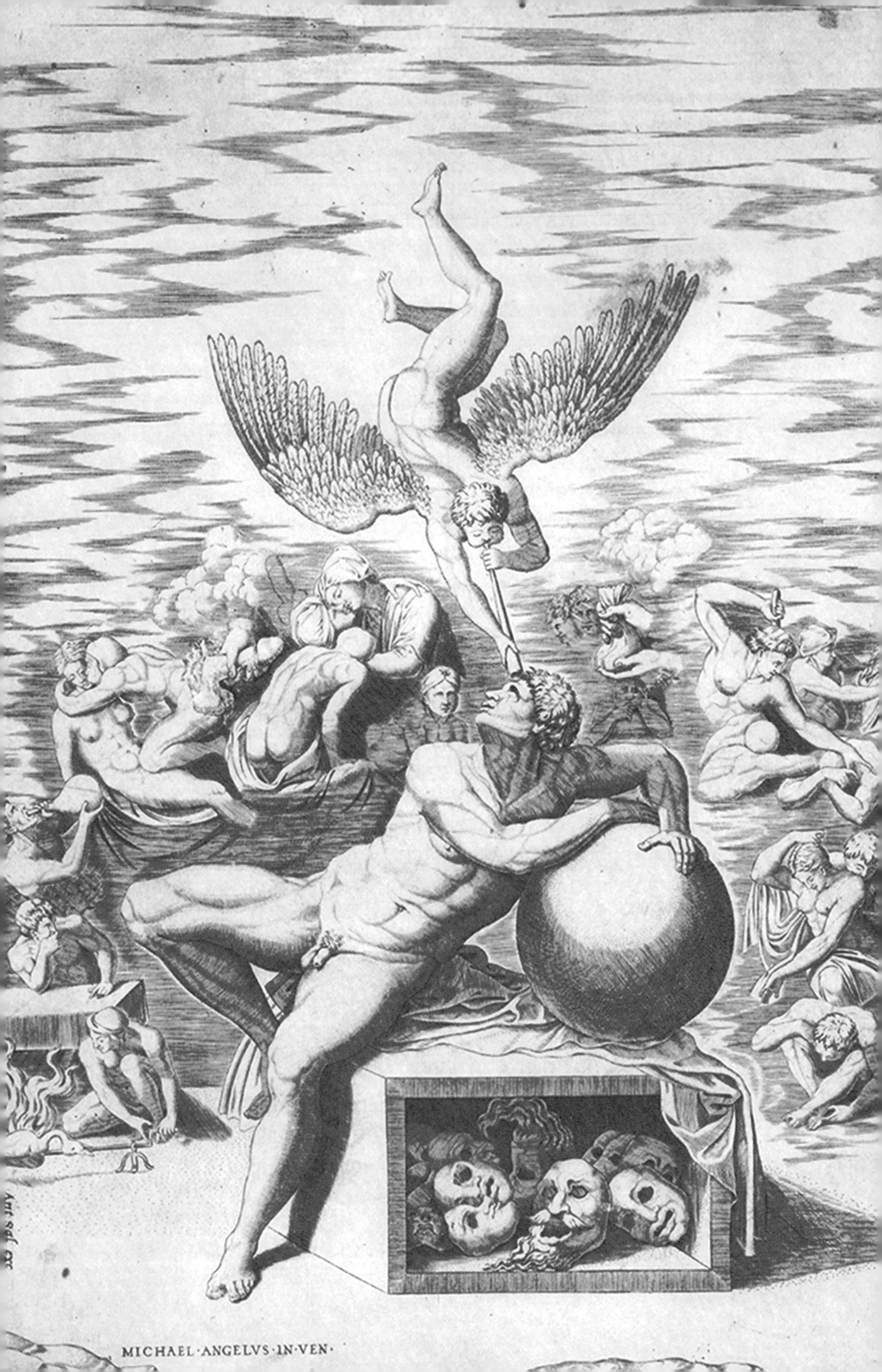
MICHAEL·ANGELVS·IN·VEN·

Ein anderer Vorschlag ist der, zu schlafen und zu träumen. Während wir uns von Äußerungen politischer Natur zurückhalten können, während wir uns selbst zum Schweigen bringen oder zum Schweigen gebracht werden können, kann niemand unsere Träume zum Schweigen bringen, während wir schlafen. Schlafen ist ein natürlicher Prozess der Wiederbelebung, in dem aktive Erneuerung, Verjüngung, das Zurückgewinnen von Kraft und die Verarbeitung des Seele-Körper-Verhältnisses stattfinden. Im Schlaf werden zudem unsere Erfahrungen verarbeitet, und Informationen, die aufgenommen wurden, werden aufbereitet und im Lang- oder Kurzzeitgedächtnis festgehalten.

Wie können wir Schlaf und Traum als Räume und sogar als Taten des unbewussten politischen Widerstands sehen? Hier muss man über den bürgerlichen Begriff des Widerstandes durch den Schlaf als Abstinenz hinausblicken, da dies nur möglich ist, wenn man das Privileg hat, über Ressourcen für den Lebensunterhalt zu verfügen. Außerdem erinnert Schlafen in einem solchen Kontext eher an den Prozess des Zum-Schweigen-Bringens oder

Another proposition is sleeping and dreaming. While we can all restrain ourselves from utterances of political nature, while we can silence ourselves and be silenced, no one can silence our dreams while we sleep. Sleep is a natural process of resuscitation, during which active restoration, rejuvenation, regaining of strengths and reprocessing of the mind-body take place. It is also in sleep that our experiences are processed, and information taken on are processed and consolidated in short- to long-term memory. How can we consider sleep and dreaming as spaces and even as acts of/for unconscious political resistance? Here, one has to look beyond the bourgeoisie concept of resistance through sleep as abstinence, as this is only possible if one enjoys the privilege of possessing the resources for sustenance. Also, sleep within such a context is reminiscent to silencing or being silenced rather than a subversion.

It is more intriguing to consider how sleeping, or taking the time to sleep matters, especially within a neoliberal economic context of productivity and over-productivity, and within a social context

Zum-Schweigen-gebracht-Werdens als an Subversion.

Es ist interessant zu untersuchen, welche Bedeutung Schlaf oder sich die Zeit zum Schlafen zu nehmen, zukommt, vor allem in einem neoliberalen wirtschaftlichen Kontext der Produktivität und Überproduktivität und in einem sozialen Kontext, in dem Drogen zur Verfügung stehen, mit denen man tagelang ohne Schlaf auskommen kann. Innerhalb eines solchen Rahmens wird das Schlafen zum wirtschaftlichen, sozialen und politischen Widerstand, sich die Zeit zum Schlafen zu nehmen wird zu einer Handlung, die Einschübe in überlastete und überregulierte Systeme schafft, und das Ausruhen wird zu einem Akt der Nichtkooperation mit diesen Systemen. Das Schlafen ist zudem ein kollektiver Akt, der von Millionen Menschen auf der ganzen Welt zu jeder gegebenen Zeit geteilt wird. Eine Gemeinschaft von Schlafenden. Es ist ein Moment des Teilens von Verjüngung, aber auch ein Moment des Teilens von Verwundbarkeit und der Aufgabe seiner Selbst in der Fürsorge anderer, wie Siobhan Phillips in »Sleep as Resistance. Hejinian, Whitman, and the politics of sleep«[4] argu-

wherein one finds drugs that allow one to go on and on for days without sleep. Within such frameworks, sleeping becomes an economic, social and political resistance, taking off time to sleep becomes an act of creating parenthesis within overloaded and over-regulated systems, and rest becomes an act of non-cooperation with those systems. Also, sleeping is a collective act shared by millions around the world at any given time.

A community of sleepers. It is a moment of sharing rejuvenation, but also a moment of sharing vulnerability and giving up one's self to the care of others, as Siobhan Phillips points out in »Sleep as Resistance: Hejinian, Whitman, and the politics of sleep«.[4] Phillips indicates, amongst other very pertinent remarks, that sleep seems to remove us from the general tyranny of the advancing clock, sleep defines time, as it divides day and night, in sleep, our brains decide what to retain and dispose of. Then he comes to the sheer fact of sleep as a deliberate choice—a political choice, which could be a mode of resistance that resuscitates sociality.

4 Siobhan Phillips, Sleep as Resistance: Hejinian, Whitman, and the politics of sleep, 2014, available via https://www.poetryfoundation.org/features/articles/detail/70108 (retrieved 10.01.2017).

mentiert. Phillips weist u.a. darauf hin, dass Schlaf uns von der allgemeinen Tyrannei der tickenden Uhr zu befreien scheint, Schlaf definiert Zeit, da er Tag und Nacht teilt; im Schlaf entscheidet unser Gehirn, was behalten und was entsorgt wird. Dann kommt er zu der schieren Tatsache des Schlafens als eine bewusste Entscheidung – eine politische Entscheidung, die ein Modus des Widerstands sein könnte, der Sozialität wiederbelebt.

(…)

Die elenden Gesichter von Lebensmüden, die weißen Mienen von Leichen, die fahlen Gesichter von Trinkern, die kränklich-grauen Gesichter von Onanisten,
Die klaffenden Leiber auf Schlachtfeldern, die Irren in ihren stark verschlossenen Zellen, die heiligen Narren, die Neugeborenen, aus Pforten sich drängend, und die Sterbenden, aus Pforten sich drängend,
Die Nacht überwältigt sie und hüllt sie ein.

(…)

Die Blinden schlafen, und die Taubstummen schlafen,
Der Gefangene schläft fest im Gefängnis, der entlaufene Sohn schläft,
Der Mörder, der am nächsten Tag gehenkt werden soll, wie schläft er?
Und der Ermordete, wie schläft er?

(…)

(…)

The wretched features of ennuyes, the white features of corpses, the livid faces of drunkards, the sick-gray faces of onanists,
The gash'd bodies on battle-fields, the insane in their
strong-door'd rooms, the sacred idiots, the new-born emerging from gates, and the dying emerging from gates,
The night pervades them and infolds them.

(…)

The blind sleep, and the deaf and dumb sleep,
The prisoner sleeps well in the prison, the runaway son sleeps,
The murderer that is to be hung next day, how does he sleep?
And the murder'd person, how does he sleep?

(…)

I go from bedside to bedside, I sleep close with the other sleepers
each in turn,
I dream in my dream all the dreams of the other dreamers,
And I become the other dreamers.

(…)

I am the actor, the actress, the voter, the politician,
The emigrant and the exile, the criminal that stood in the box,
He who has been famous and he who shall be famous after to-day,
The stammerer, the well-form'd person, the wasted or feeble person.

(…)

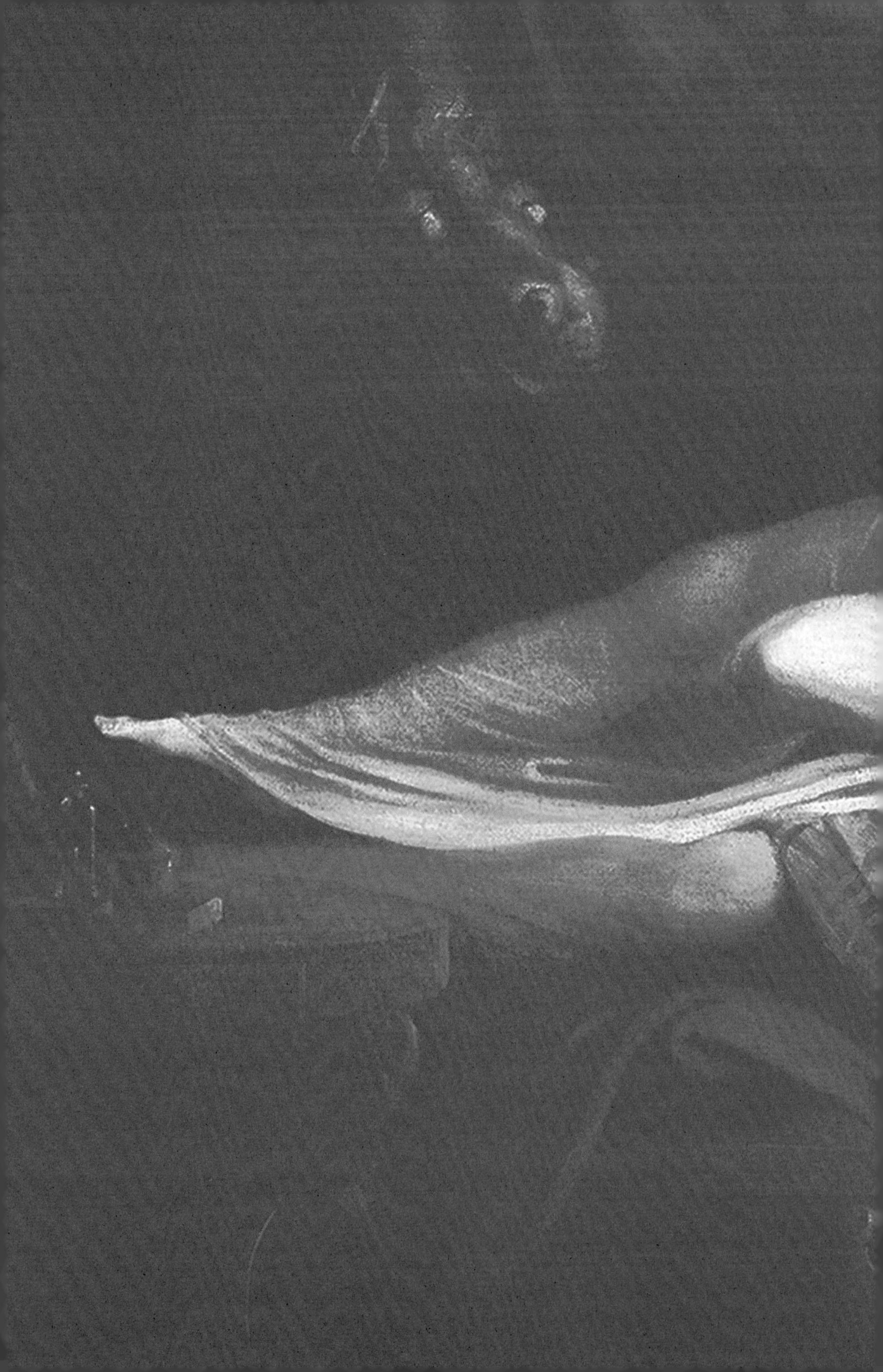

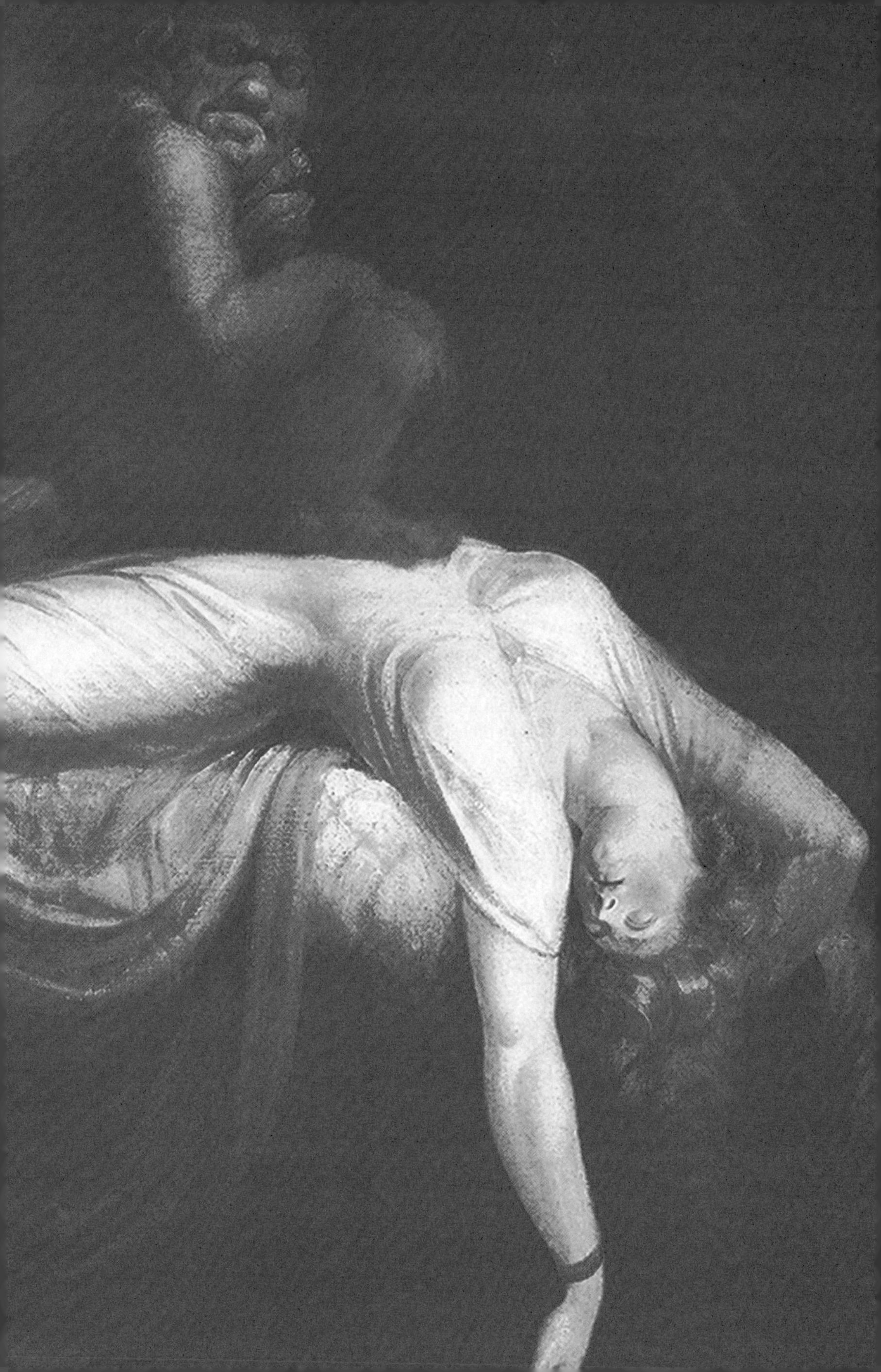

34

Ich gehe von Bettstatt zu Bettstatt,
ich schlafe dicht bei den Schläfern,
einem nach dem andern,
Ich träume in meinem Traum alle
Träume der andern Träumer,
Und ich selbst bin die andern Träumer.

(...)

Ich bin der Schauspieler, die Schau-
spielerin, der Wähler, der Politiker,
Der Auswanderer und der Verbannte,
der Verbrecher,
der hinterm Gitter stand,
Bin der, der berühmt war, und der
morgen berühmt sein wird,
Der Stotterer, der Wohlgestaltete,
der Zerstörte und Schwache.

(...)

O Liebe und Sommer, ihr seid in den
Träumen und in mir,
Herbst und Winter sind in den Träu-
men, der Farmer träumt von der Farm,
Die Herden und Saaten gedeihen, die
Scheunen sind wohlgefüllt.

Elemente verschmelzen mit der
Nacht, Schiffe lavieren in
Träumen,
Der Seemann segelt, der Verbannte
kehrt heim,
Der Flüchtling kehrt wohlbehalten
heim, der Auswanderer ist wieder zu
Haus nach Monaten und Jahren,
Der arme Irländer lebt in dem
schlichten Haus seiner Kindheit mit
den vertrauten Nachbargesichtern,
Sie heißen ihn herzlich willkommen,
er ist wieder barfüßig, er vergisst,
dass er wohlhabend ist,
Der Holländer reist heim, der Schotte
und der Walliser reisen heim, und der
vom Mittelmeer stammt, reist heim,
In jeden Hafen Englands, Frankreichs,
Spaniens kehren gefüllte Schiffe,

O love and summer, you are in the
dreams and in me,
Autumn and winter are in the dreams,
the farmer goes with his thrift,
The droves and crops increase, the
barns are well-fill'd.

Elements merge in the night, ships
make tacks in the dreams,
The sailor sails, the exile returns home,
The fugitive returns unharm'd, the
immigrant is back beyond months
and years,
The poor Irishman lives in the simple
house of his childhood with
the well known neighbors and faces,
They warmly welcome him, he is bare-
foot again, he forgets he is well off,
The Dutchman voyages home, and
the Scotchman and Welshman voyage
home, and the native of the Mediter-
ranean voyages home,
To every port of England, France,
Spain, enter well-fill'd ships,
The Swiss foots it toward his hills, the
Prussian goes his way, the
Hungarian his way, and the Pole his way,
The Swede returns, and the Dane and
Norwegian return.

(...)

The sleepers are very beautiful as
they lie unclothed,
They flow hand in hand over the
whole earth from east to west as
they lie unclothed,
The Asiatic and African are hand in
hand, the European and American
are hand in hand,
Learn'd and unlearn'd are hand in
hand, and male and female are hand
in hand,
The bare arm of the girl crosses the
bare breast of her lover, they
press close without lust, his lips press
her neck,

Der Schweizer wandert zu Fuß zu seinen Bergen, der Preuße geht seinen Weg, der Ungar geht seinen Weg und der Pole geht seinen Weg,
Der Schwede kehrt heim und der Däne und Norweger kehren heim.

(...)

Die Schläfer sind sehr schön, wie sie entkleidet liegen,
Sie fluten Hand in Hand über die ganze Erde von Osten nach Westen, wie sie entkleidet liegen,
Die aus Asien und aus Afrika Hand in Hand, Europäer und Amerikaner, Hand in Hand,
Weise und Volk, Hand in Hand,
Männer und Weiber, Hand in Hand,
Der bloße Arm des Mädchens liegt über der bloßen Brust ihres Geliebten, sie schmiegen sich aneinander ohne Begier, seine Lippen küssen ihren Nacken,
Der Vater hält seinen erwachsenen oder unmündigen Sohn in seinen Armen mit unermesslicher Liebe, und der Sohn hält den Vater in seinen Armen mit unermesslicher Liebe (...)

Walt Whitman, »Die Schläfer«[5] (Auszüge), 1855

Walt Whitmans sehr langes und anspruchsvolles Gedicht »Die Schläfer« gewährt uns einen Zugang zu den Universen dieser sich verjüngenden Communitys. Das Werk an sich ist ein Ausdruck von demokratischen Idealen, Empathie und Assoziationen und für ein Gedicht aus dem Jahre 1855 der Widerstand schlechthin. Aber der

The father holds his grown or ungrown son in his arms with measureless love, and the son holds the father in his arms with measureless love (...)

Walt Whitman, »The Sleepers«[5] (excerpts), 1855

Walt Whitman's very long and sophisticated poem »The Sleepers« grants us an entry into the universes of those rejuvenating communities. The piece in itself is an expression of democratic ideals, empathies and associations, and for an 1855 piece, a resistance in itself. But the crux is how Whitman conjures political utopias within dreams and succeeds in communicating with other humans by dreaming the same dreams. Sleep becomes that space of communion, an equality of consciousness even though not all are equal, as he juxtaposes race, class, age and other social hierarchies.

The exhibition »The Name of Shades of Paranoia, Called Different Forms of Silence« is a similar proposition by Viron Erol Vert. It is the transcription of poetry into space. A space which is meant to be a dormitory qua exhibition space – a dreamatory. It is a sleeping and dreaming laboratory, clinic and factory all in one. As fear has silenced and

5 Walt Whitman, Leaves of Grass: Comprehensive Reader's Edition, Blodgett, H.W., et al. (eds.), London 1965.

Kernpunkt ist, wie Whitman politische Utopien im Traum heraufbeschwört und wie es ihm gelingt, mit anderen Menschen zu kommunizieren, indem er dieselben Träume träumt. Schlaf wird zum Ort der Gemeinschaft, zu einer Gleichheit des Bewusstseins, obwohl nicht alle gleich sind, da er »race«, »class«, Alter und andere soziale Hierarchien gegenüberstellt.

Die Ausstellung »The Name of Shades of Paranoia, Called Different Forms of Silence« ist ein ähnlicher Vorschlag von Viron Erol Vert. Sie ist die Transkription der Poesie in den Raum. Ein Raum, der als Schlafsaal qua Ausstellungsraum gedacht ist – ein Dreamatory. Es ist ein Schlaf-und-Traum-Labor, Klinik und Fabrik in einem. Da Angst die Menschen zum Schweigen gebracht und ihnen sowohl den Ort als auch die Mittel des Sich-zum-Ausdruck-Bringens genommen hat, schlägt Vert in diesem Projekt einen Raum vor, in den die Menschen kommen können, um zu schlafen.

Der Vorsatz ist hierbei von entscheidender Bedeutung. Es ist der Akt des Sich-Zeit-Nehmens von der Tyrannei des Alltags, der ein Wider-

deprived people of spaces and the right words and voices to express themselves, Vert in this project proposes a space wherein people can come by to catch some sleep. The deliberateness in this is crucial. It is this taking time off the tyranny of the quotidian which is the resistance to the system.

Within this space furnished with beds, sound and a conducive sleeping outfit, Vert creates a democratic space wherein old and young, rich and poor, native and foreigner can come together and share dreams. On the one hand, sharing dreams in a Whitmanian sense, i.e. dreaming other people's dreams, and on the other hand sharing dreams by narrating what they dreamt about.

Vert aims at transforming the space of Galerie Wedding into a cocoon or a womb that insinuates a safe haven. People can come in on a daily basis to narrate the dreams they had last night, or they might choose to have a siesta, and share their dreams if they remember. On an irregular basis, oneirocritics will be invited to the gallery space to interpret some dreams upon request by the dreamers. On

stand gegen das System ist. Mit diesem Raum, der mit Betten, Klängen und einem gewissen Komfort ausgestattet ist, schafft Vert einen demokratischen Raum, in dem sich alte und junge, reiche und arme, eingeborene und zugezogene Menschen zusammenfinden und Träume teilen können. Einerseits teilen sie Träume im Sinne Whitmans, das Träumen der Träume anderer Menschen, auf der anderen Seite teilen sie sich gegenseitig mit, was sie geträumt haben.

Vert möchte die Galerie Wedding in einen Kokon oder eine Gebärmutter verwandeln, die einen sicheren Zufluchtsort darstellt. Die Leute können täglich vorbeikommen, um ihre Träume aus der letzten Nacht zu erzählen, oder sie können eine Siesta machen und anschließend ihre Träume erzählen, falls sie sich erinnern. In unregelmäßigen Abständen werden Traumdeuter in den Galerieraum eingeladen, um auf Wunsch die Träume zu interpretieren. Täglich wird ein Traum des Tages ausgewählt und veröffentlicht.

»The Name of Shades of Paranoia, Called Different Forms of Silence« bemüht sich,

a daily basis a dream of the day will be selected and published in some form.

»The Name of Shades of Paranoia, Called Different Forms of Silence« is an effort to convoke other spaces of sociopolitical reflections and resistances, in particular within the realm of the subconscious of sleeping and dreaming. A space where unfearing and un-silencing are explored and practiced.

The project will also acknowledge the fact that although everyone dreams, metaphorical dreaming and the ability to remember one's dreams, are also privileges. In extreme dire straits dreams are luxuries, as they too are silenced by the sheer brutality of reality.

The exhibition project by Viron Erol Vert will be accompanied by lectures by scientists researching on dreams, as well as three performances by Driftmachine framed around three of the dream deities, Oneiroi, in Ovid's »Metamorphoses«, namely Morpheus (god of dreams), Phobetor (god of nightmares) and Phantasos (god of surreal dreams, of inanimate objects in prophetic dreams).

andere Räume gesellschaftspolitischer Reflexionen und Widerstände zusammenzubringen, insbesondere im Kontext des Unterbewusstseins von Schlaf und Traum. Ein Raum, in dem Nicht-Angst und Nicht-Schweigen erforscht und praktiziert werden.

Das Projekt »The Name of Shades of Paranoia, Called Different Forms of Silence« wird auch die Tatsache berücksichtigen, dass zwar alle träumen, aber das metaphorische Träumen und die Fähigkeit, sich an seine Träume zu erinnern, auch Privilegien sind. In extremen Notsituationen sind Träume Luxus, da sie durch die schiere Brutalität der Realität zum Schweigen gebracht werden.

Das Ausstellungsprojekt von Viron Erol Vert wird begleitet von Vorträgen von Traumforschern sowie drei Performances von Driftmachine, in denen es um die drei Traumgötter Oneiroi aus Ovids »Metamorphosen« geht, nämlich Morpheus, den Gott der Träume, Phobetor, den Gott der Albträume, und Phantasos, den Gott der surrealen Träume und der unbelebten Objekte in prophetischen Träumen.

1. Pierre Narcisse Guérin (1774–1833), Morpheus and Iris 1811, Hermitage Torrent.
2. Francisco de Goya (1746–1828), The Sleep of Reason Produces Monsters c. 1797/1798, Wellcome Library.
3. Nicolas Beatrizet (c. 1520–c. 1562) after Michelangelo, The Dream, Rijks Museum.
4. Johann Heinrich Füssli (1741–1825), The Nightmare c. 1781 vgl. S. 79 The Yorck Project 2002.
5. Bertel Thorvaldsen (1768–1844), Gipsabguss von 2006 nach dem Original in Marmor von 1815. © Photo: David Brandt.

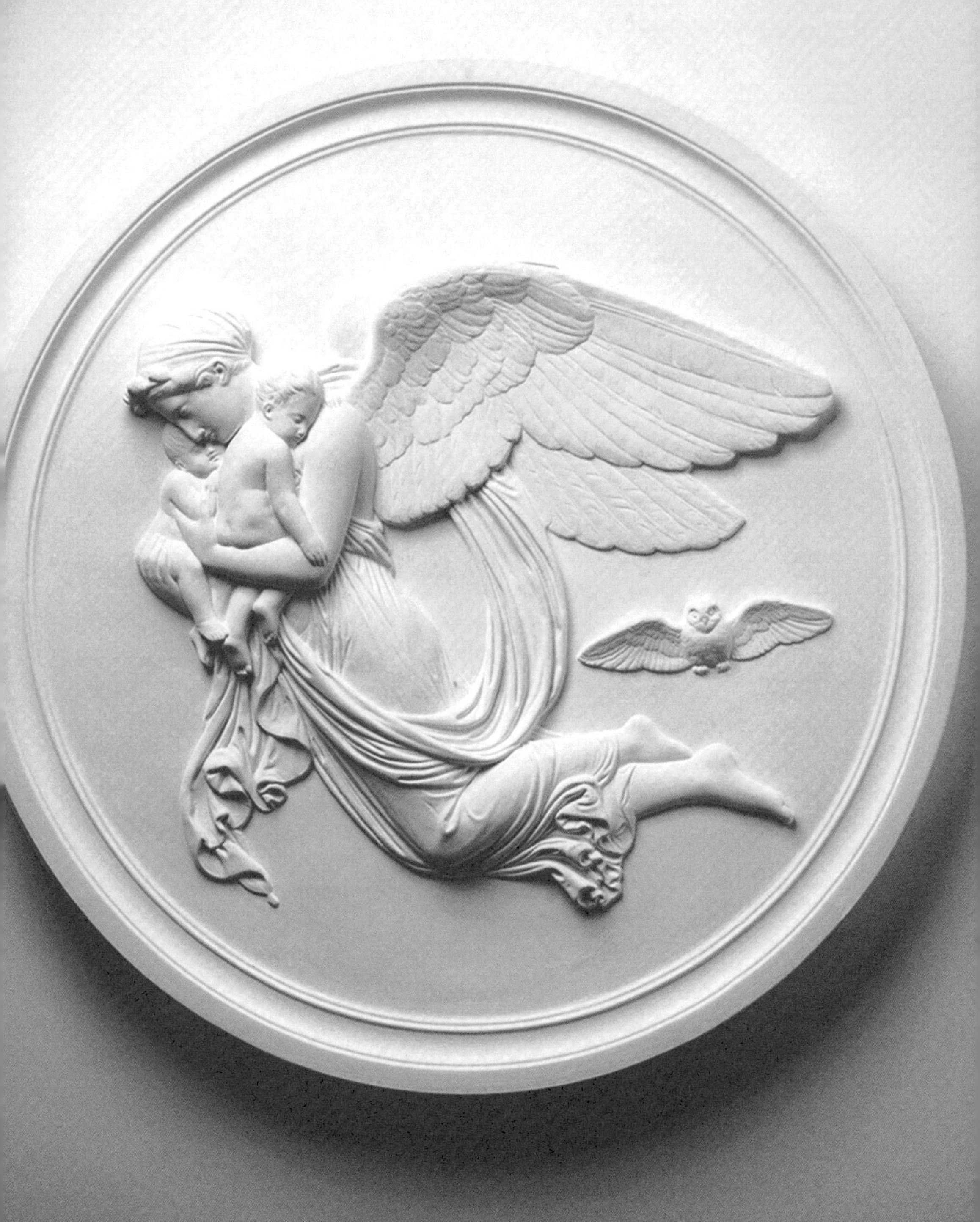

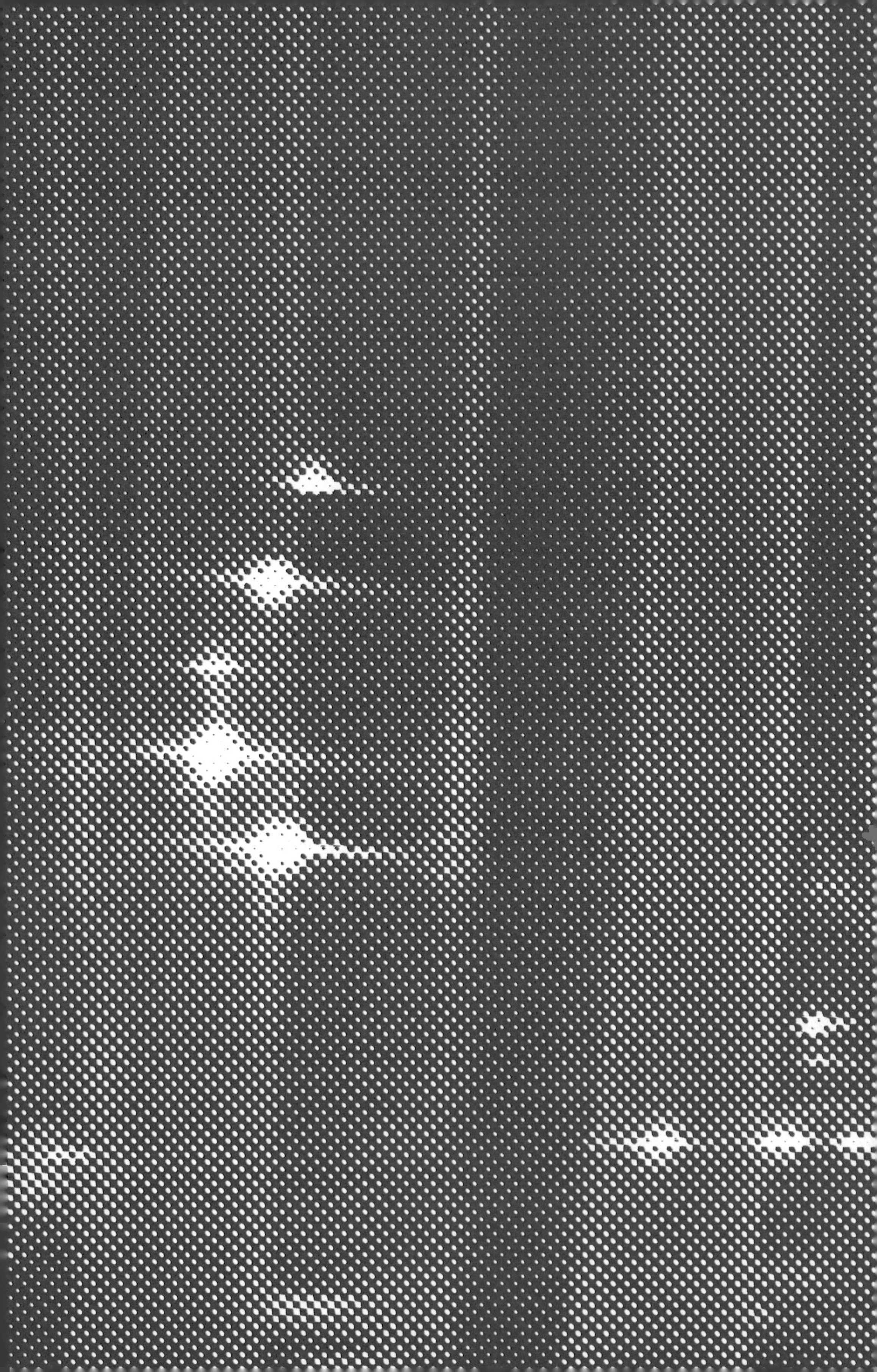

ONEIROI

DE

Drei Oneiroi – Götter des Traumes in der griechischen Mythologie – fungierten als symbolische Rahmung für das Begleitprogramm von Viron Erol Verts Ausstellung. Die Eigentümlichkeiten des Wesens und der Fähigkeiten von Morpheus, Phobetor und Phantasos wurden vom Duo Driftmachine musikalisch assoziativ aufgegriffen und zu einer Oneiroi-Trilogie verwoben. Mit dieser hüllten sie die Abende im »Dreamatory« in einen klanglichen Stimmungsteppich, was die durch Möblierung und Beleuchtung erzeugte traumfördernde Atmosphäre des Raumes noch weiter vertiefte.

EN

Three Oneiroi – the gods of dreams in Greek mythology – have functioned as symbolic framing for the programme that accompanied Viron Erol Vert's exhibition. In terms of character and ability, the duo Driftmachine has picked up the peculiarities of Morpheus, Phobetor and Phantasos in a musical associative manner in order to interweave it into a Oneiroi-trilogy. This way, and by adding a tonal mood carpet to the evenings that took place within the »Dreamatory«, the dream-enhancing atmosphere created by the furnishing and lighting has been underlined.

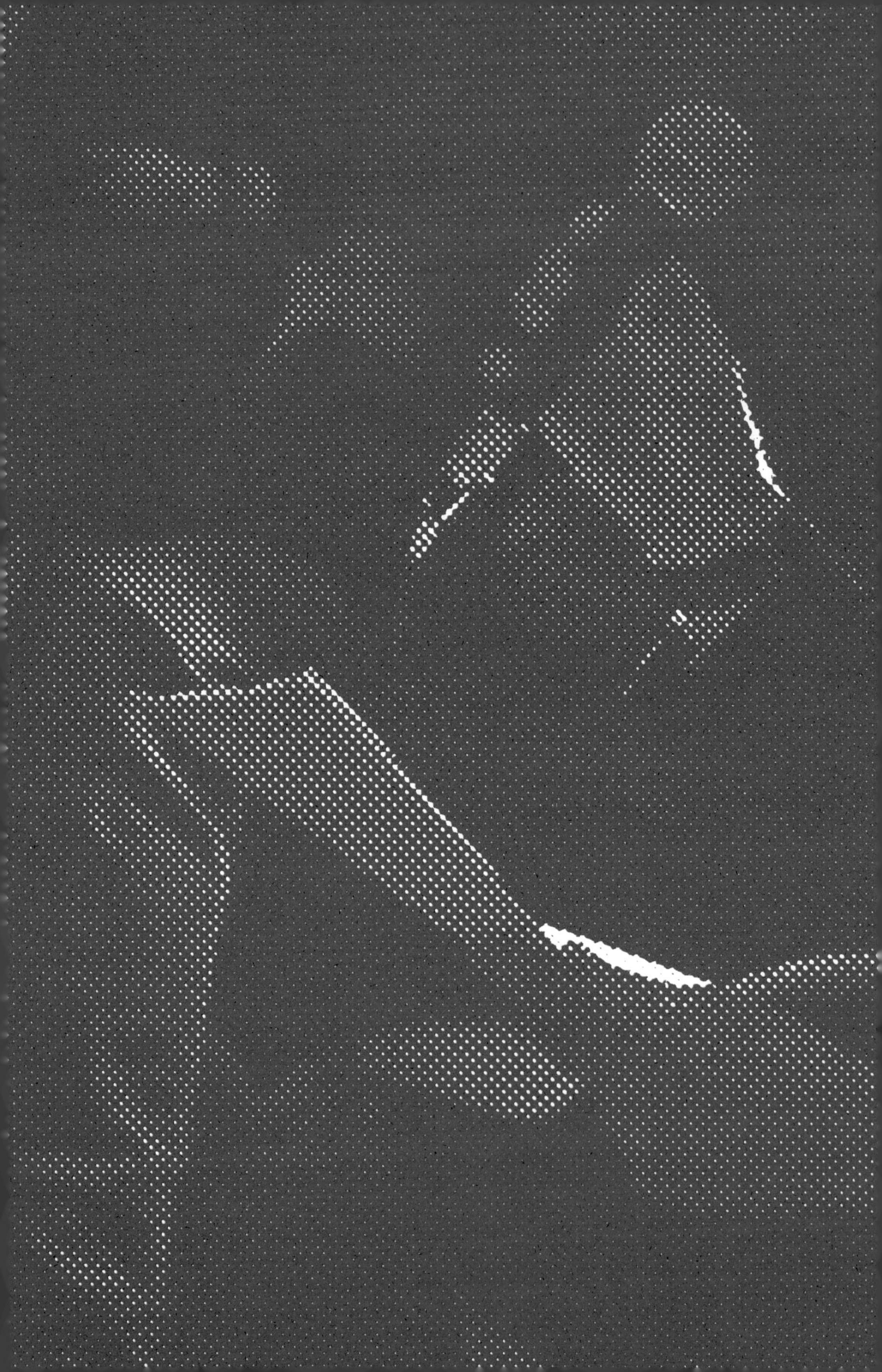

MORPHEUS

DE

Der Eröffnungsabend von »The Name of Shades of Paranoia, Called Different Forms of Silence« stand im Zeichen von Morpheus, jenem Oneiros, der im Traum menschliche Gestalt anzunehmen und die Eigenarten des menschlichen Handelns zu imitieren vermag. Das Weddinger »Dreamatory« lud erstmalig seine Besucher*innen dazu ein, seine Ausstattung zu erproben und in seine Stimmung einzutauchen. Anlässlich der Einweihung des Traumraumes kam es zur Aufführung der Oneiro Trilogy Live Performance №1 »Morpheus« von Driftmachine.

EN

The opening of »The Name of Shades of Paranoia, Called Different Forms of Silence« was much influenced by Morpheus, the Oneiros who takes human shape and imitates the peculiarities of human action within the dream. For the first time, the Wedding »Dreamatory« invited its visitors to test its facilities and to immerse in its atmosphere. To mark the inauguration of the dreamspace the Oneiro Trilogy Live Performance №1 »Morpheus« by Driftmachine took place.

http://www.umor-rex.org/ur088/

Download all Tracks

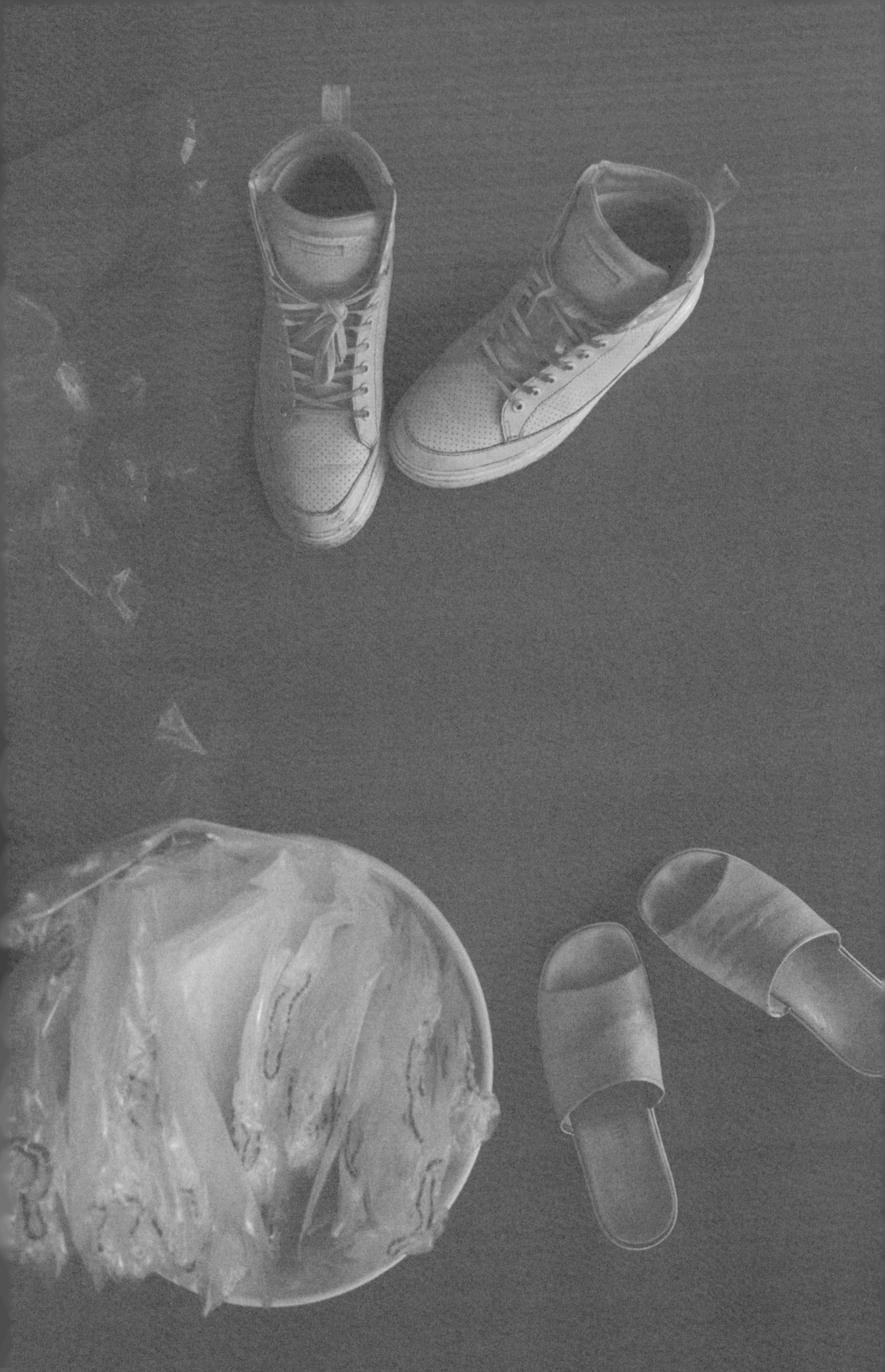

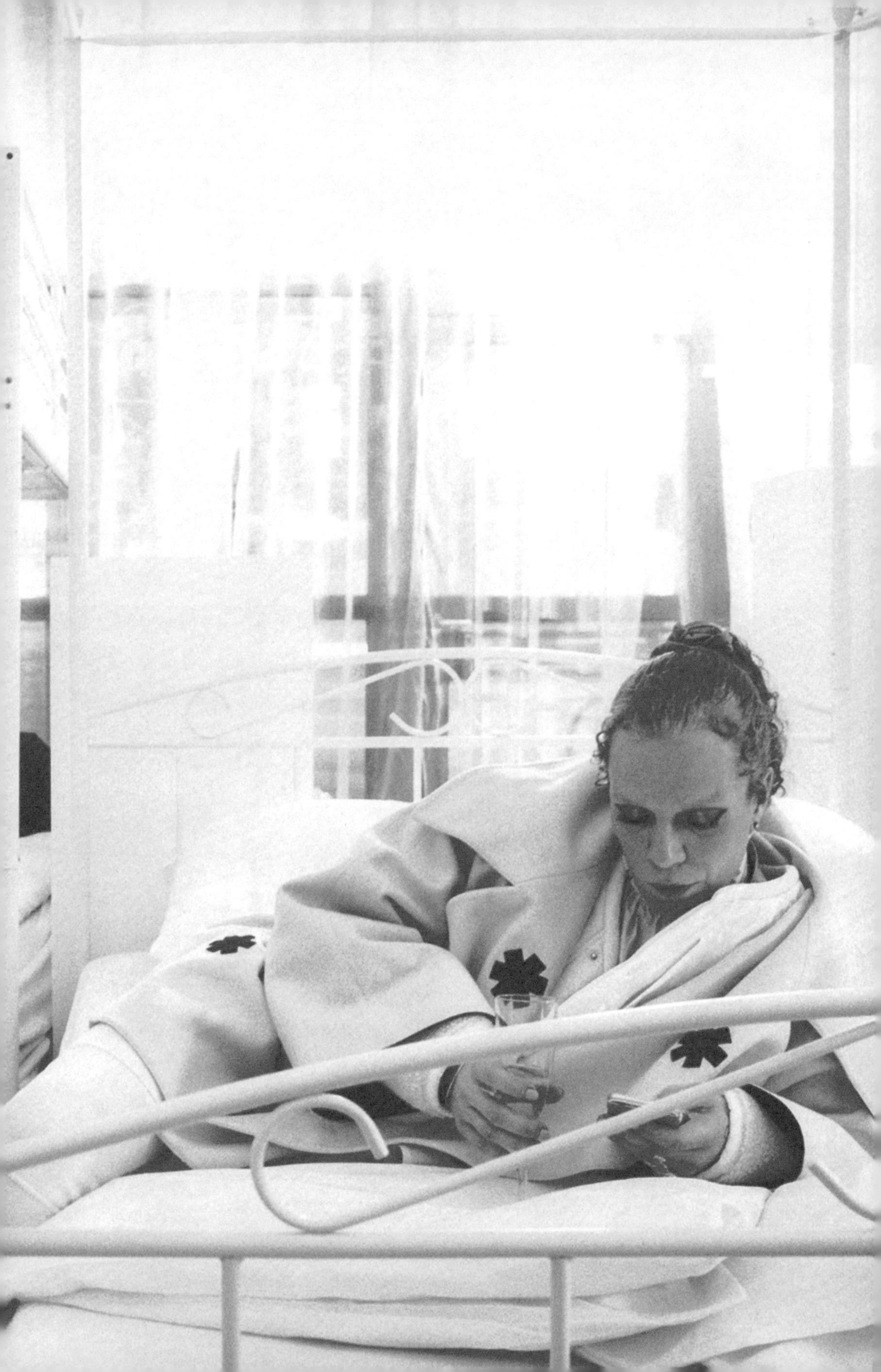

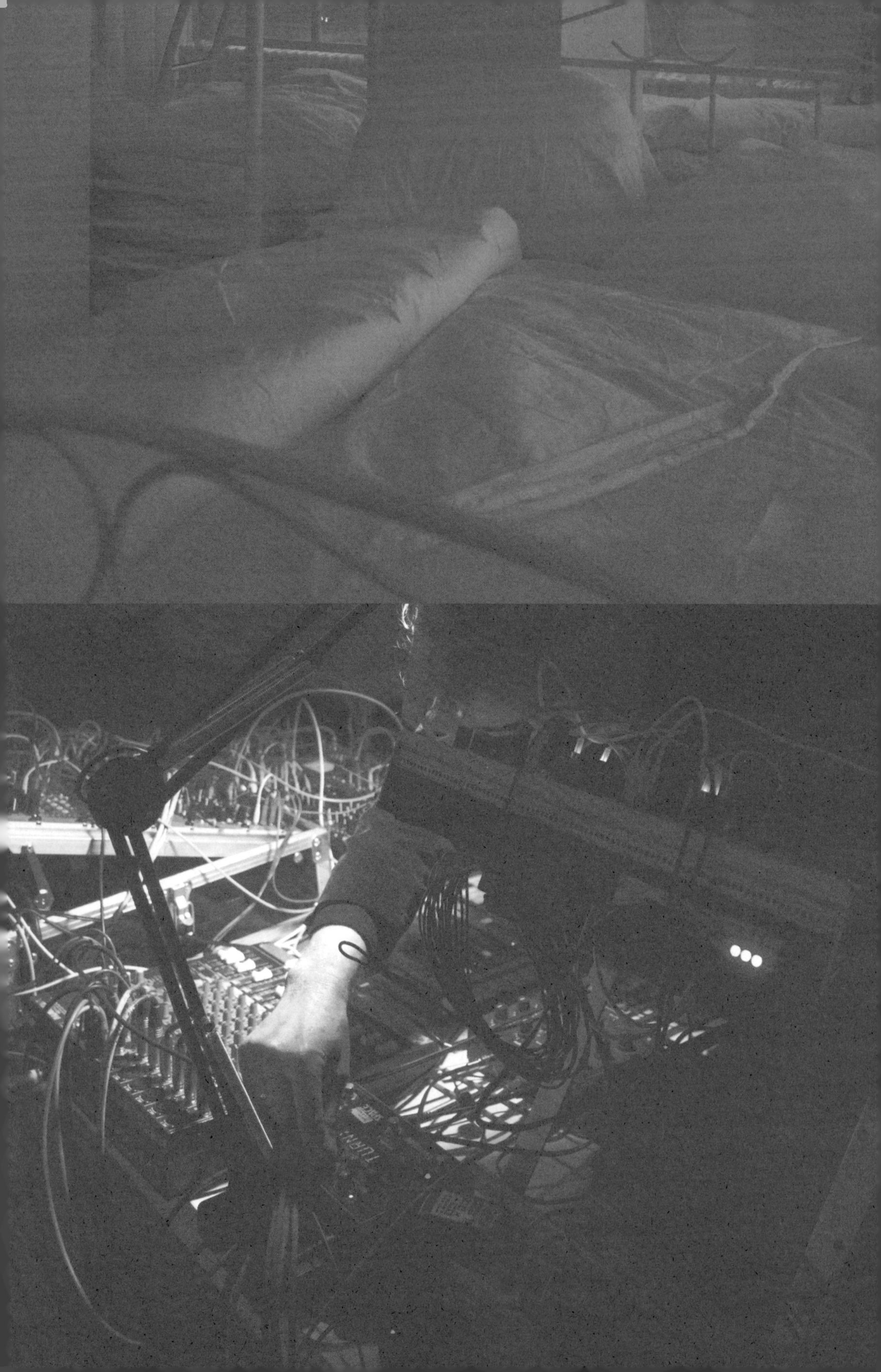

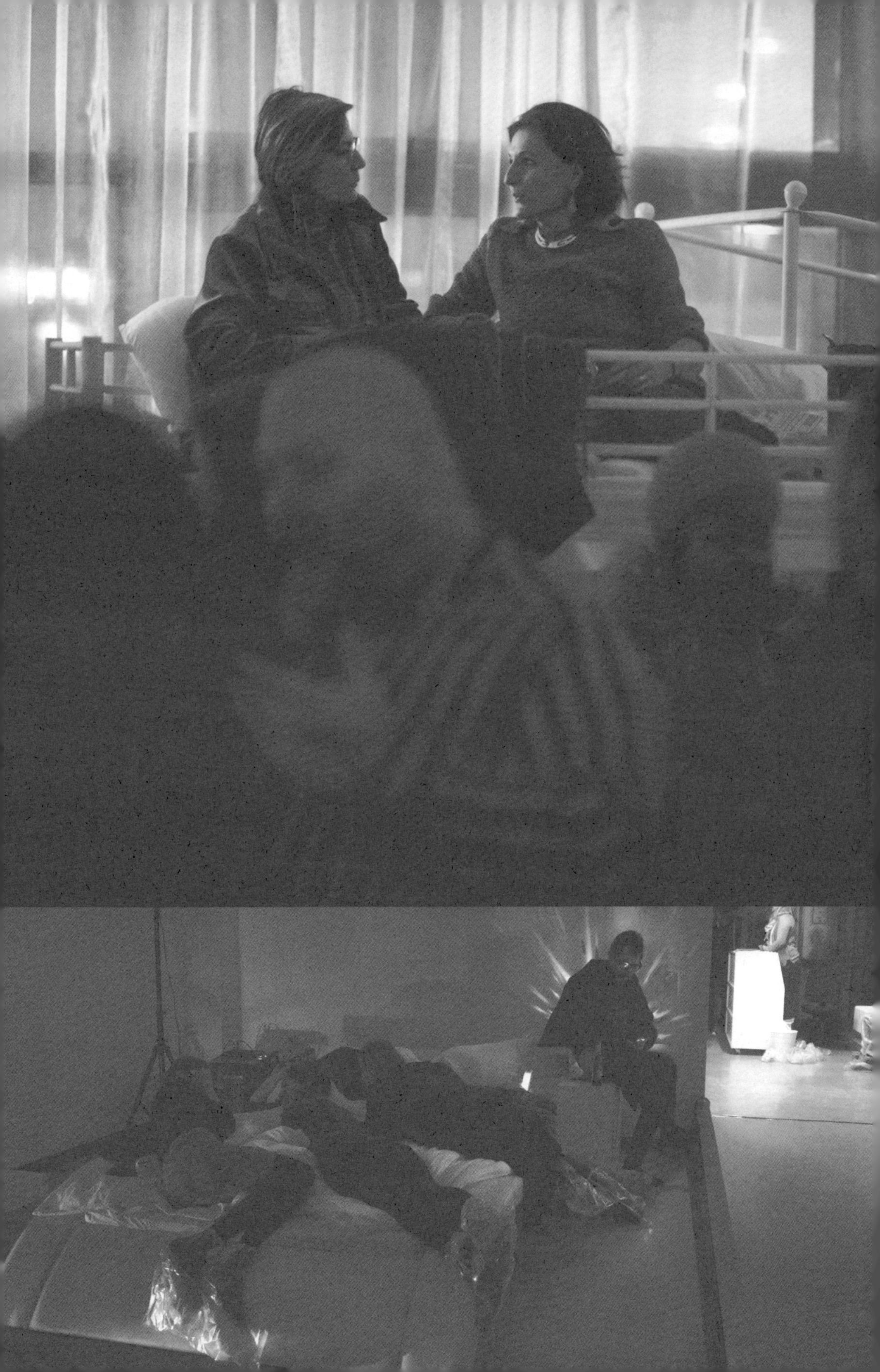

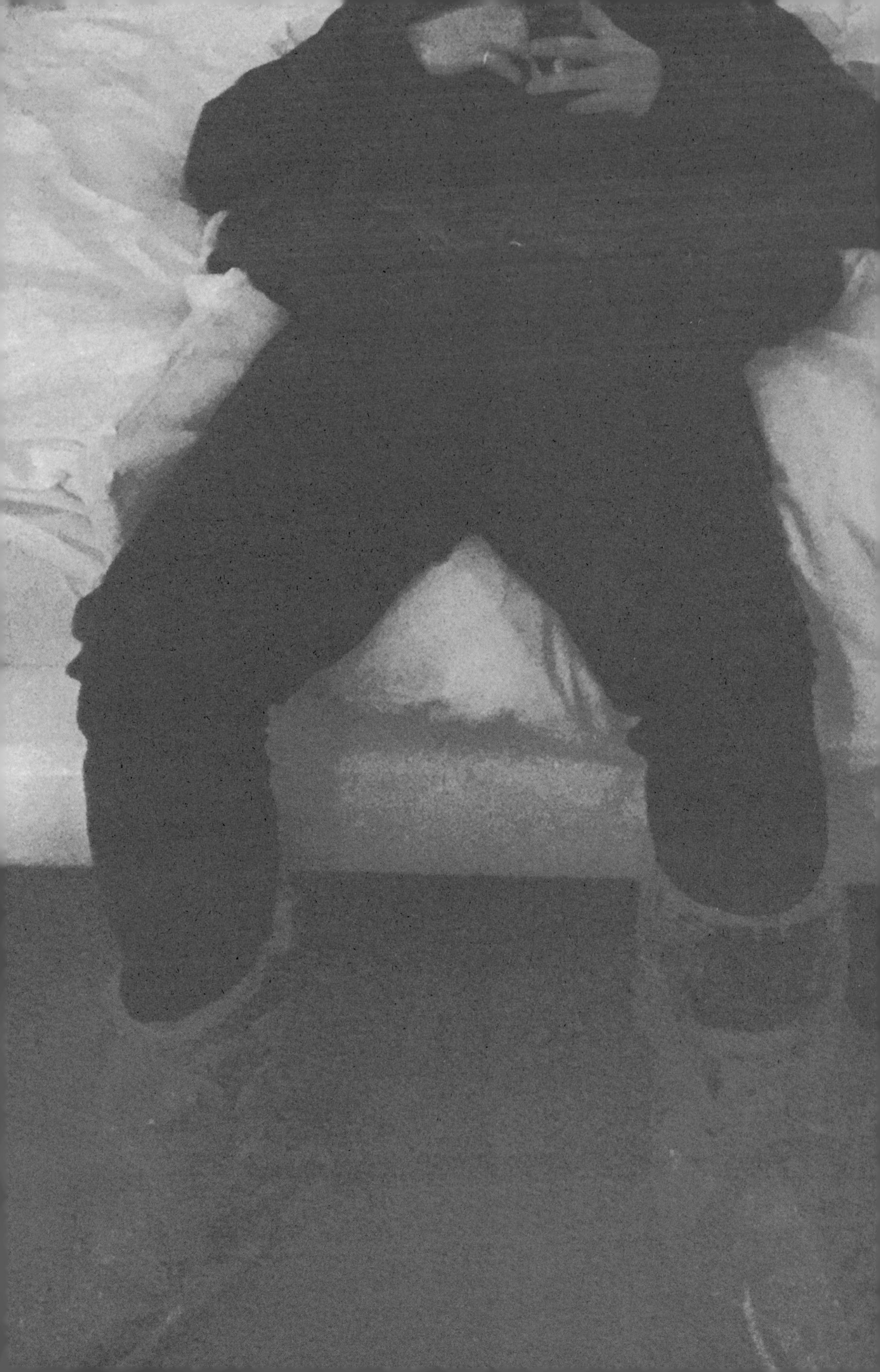

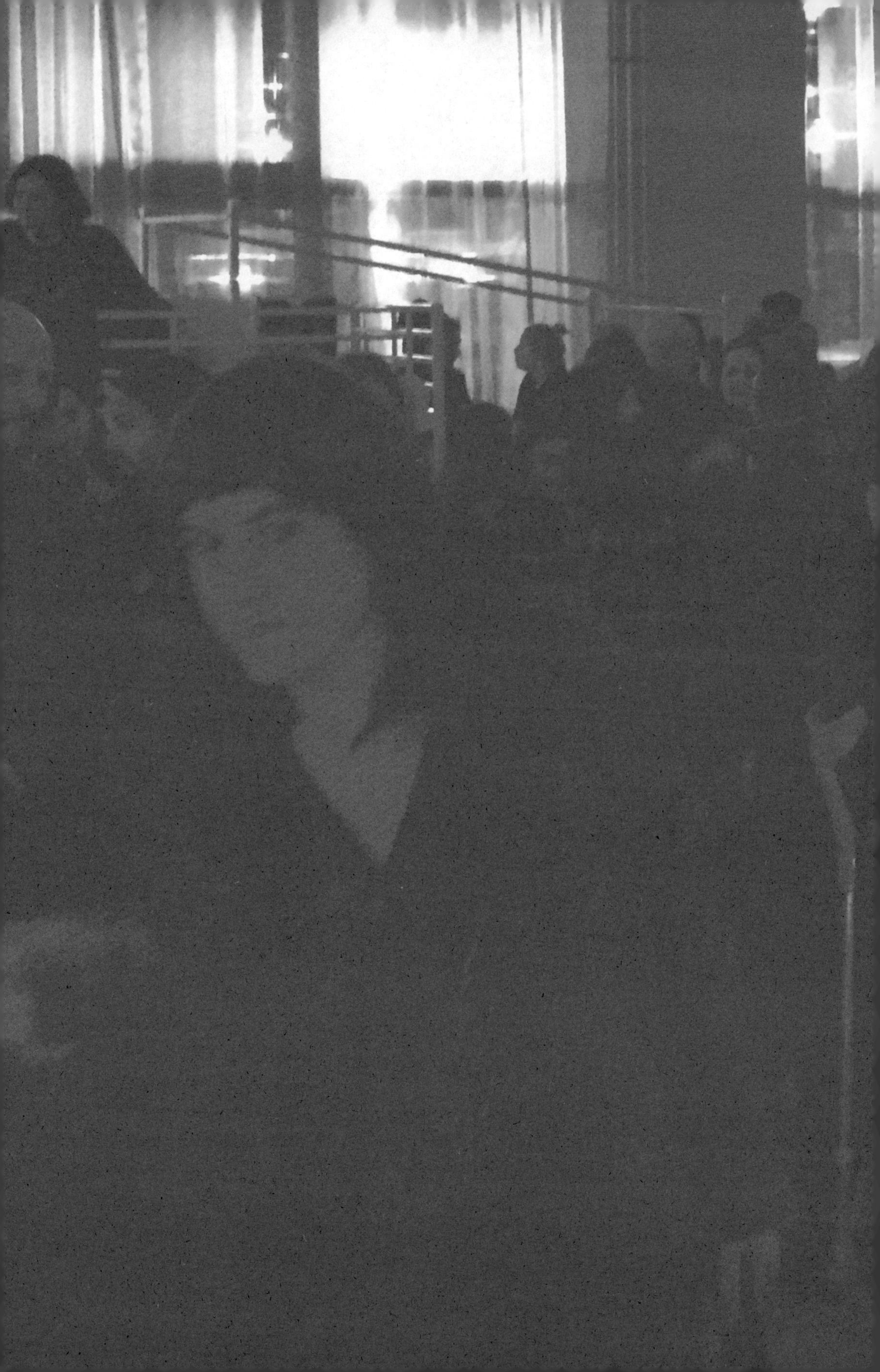

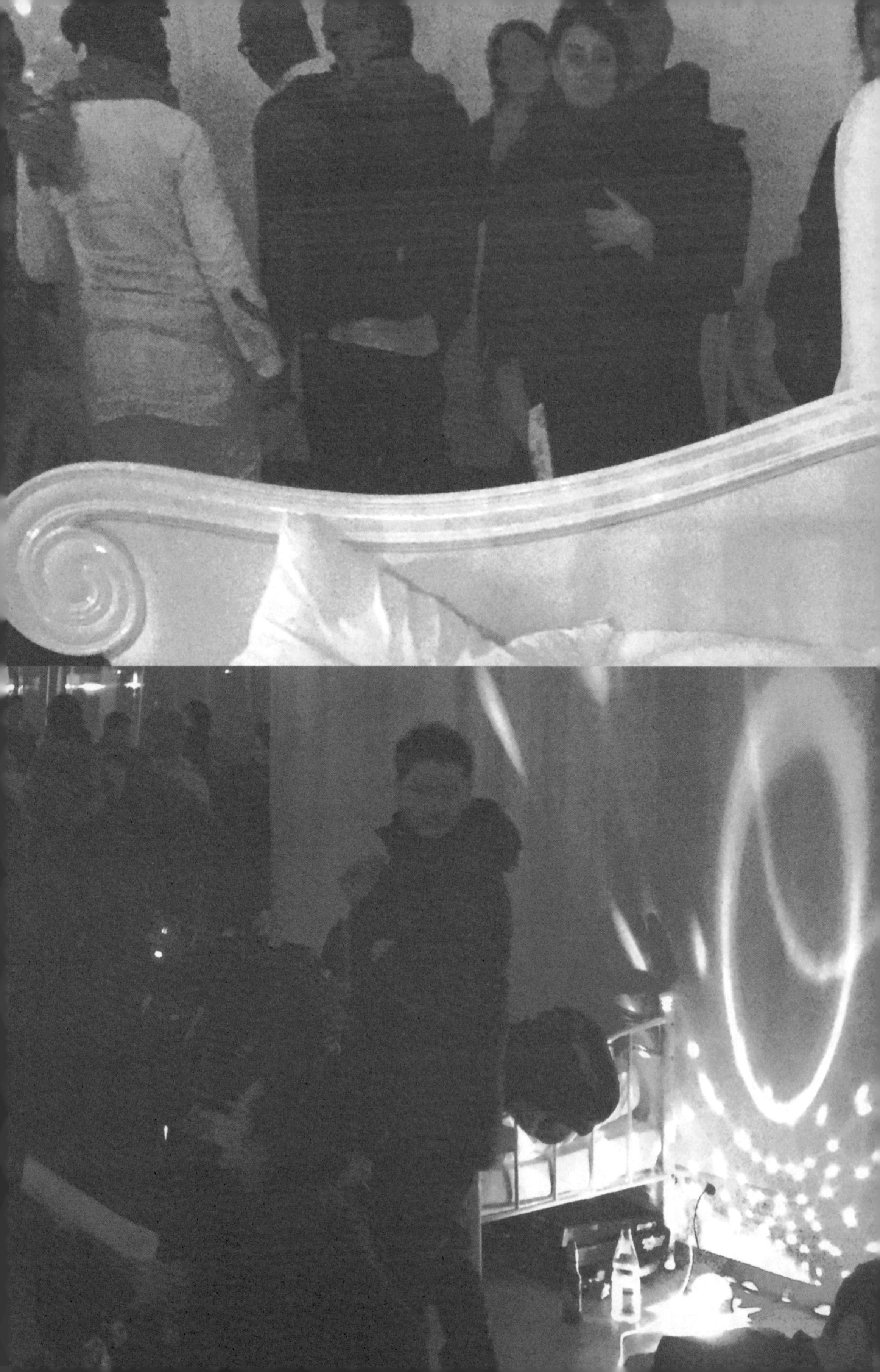

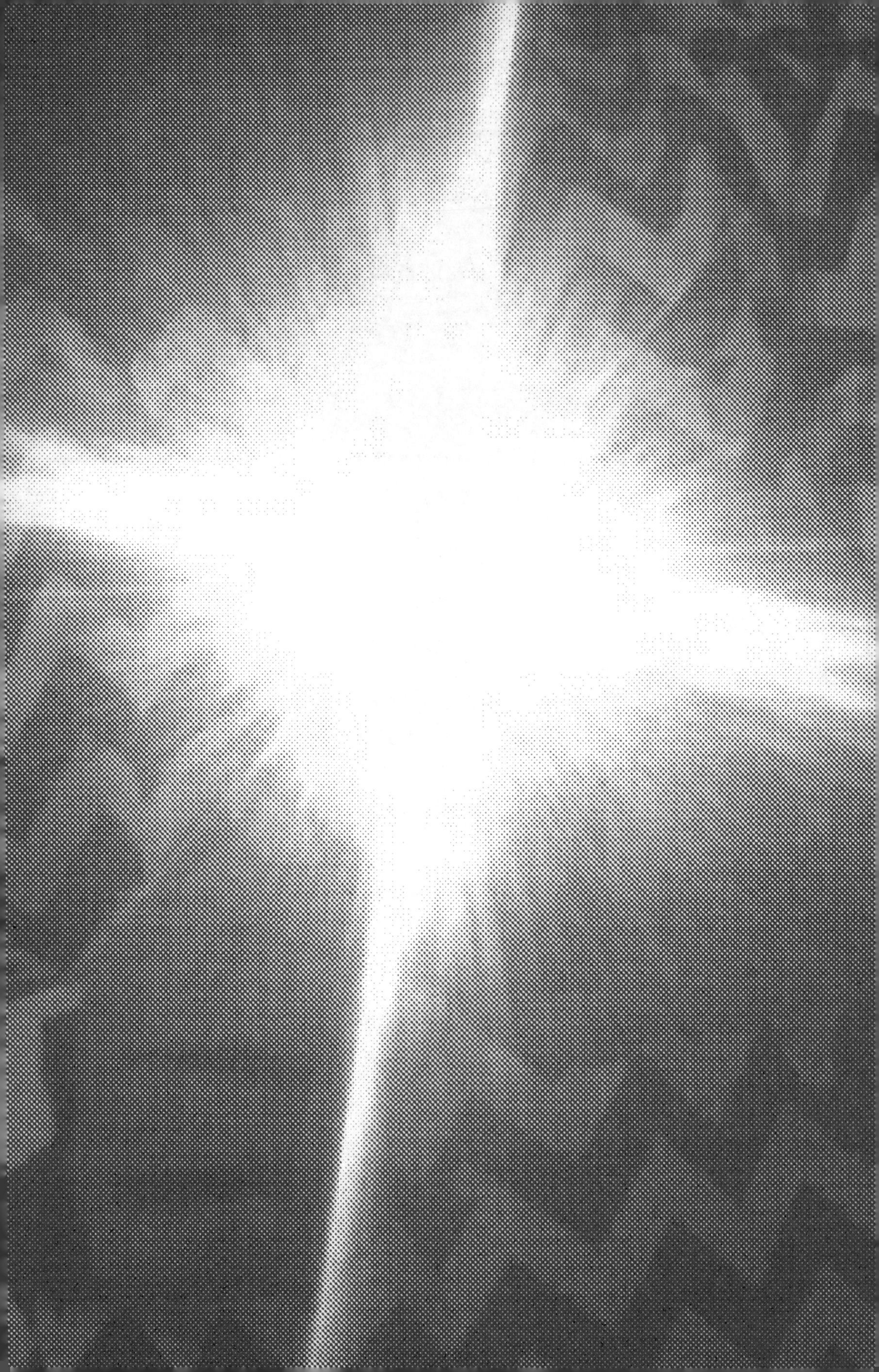

KINO MORPH

DE

Traum im Film... Wie stellt eine Industrie, die bisweilen selbst als Traumfabrik bezeichnet wird, Träume dar? Schon ein erster Überblick zeigt, dass die sogenannten Traumsequenzen in Filmen meist eine tragende Rolle spielen. Oft stehen sie am Anfang oder am Ende des Films, die Narrative initiierend oder abschließend, wenn nicht gar erklärend, häufig bilden sie eine stilisierte und komprimierte Nacherzählung der gesamten Handlung. Nicht zu unterschätzen sind dabei auch Filme, die sich nahezu komplett in der Traumwelt abspielen. Ob nun Freudianisch erklärt oder musikalisch verklärt, gemein haben diese Sequenzen fast immer, dass Regie und Ausstattung sich hier ausleben können. Oft werden Personen von außerhalb mit der Gestaltung der Szenen beauftragt, um auf diese Weise dem Film eine neue Ebene von Fremdartig-

EN

Dreams in movies... How can an industry so often referred to as the dream factory depict dreams? Research has already shown that so-called dream sequences often play a fundamental part in films. Often they take place in the beginning or the end of the film, initiating or concluding, if not telling the narrative, and frequently form a stylised and condensed re-production of the story-line. There are also many movies that are (almost) entirely set in the dream world. Regardless of whether they're viewed through a rationalised-Freudian lens or transfigured into musical numbers, they typically form the parts of films, which allow the (art) directors to really run free... Often people from outside of the industry are invited to shape these scenes to breathe a truly unfamiliar air into the film: visions from another world, a world the protagonists (and we the spectators) can only dream of...

keit hinzuzufügen: Visionen einer anderen Welt, so wie die Protagonist*innen (und wir, die Zuschauer*innen) sie eben nur träumen können... Mit einer kurzweiligen, unterhaltsamen und auch ein bisschen irren Collage aus repräsentativen Traumsequenzen und Filmszenen, in denen es um Träume geht, laden wir an diesem Abend zu einer Reise durch das Unterbewusstsein selbst fiktiver Charaktere ein. Von Prä-Bollywood zu Post-Modern, von Oz zu Wiz, von Tagtraum zu Albtraum geht die Reise durch Nebelmaschinenschwaden, Massentanzszenen, romantische, blasphemische, ja

With this small, entertaining and at times off-the-wall collage of representative dream sequences as well as scenes about dreams themselves, we invite you to embark on a journey into the subconscious of fictional characters. From pre-Bollywood to post-modern, from Oz to Wiz, from daydream to nightmare, we take a trip through fog machine clouds, dance scenes of the masses, romantic, blasphemous or even mass-scale choreographies – sometimes flickering, sometimes softly blending; sometimes absurd, sometimes abstruse; sometimes bloody, sometimes smoochy; sometimes innova-

film collage © Yusuf Etiman

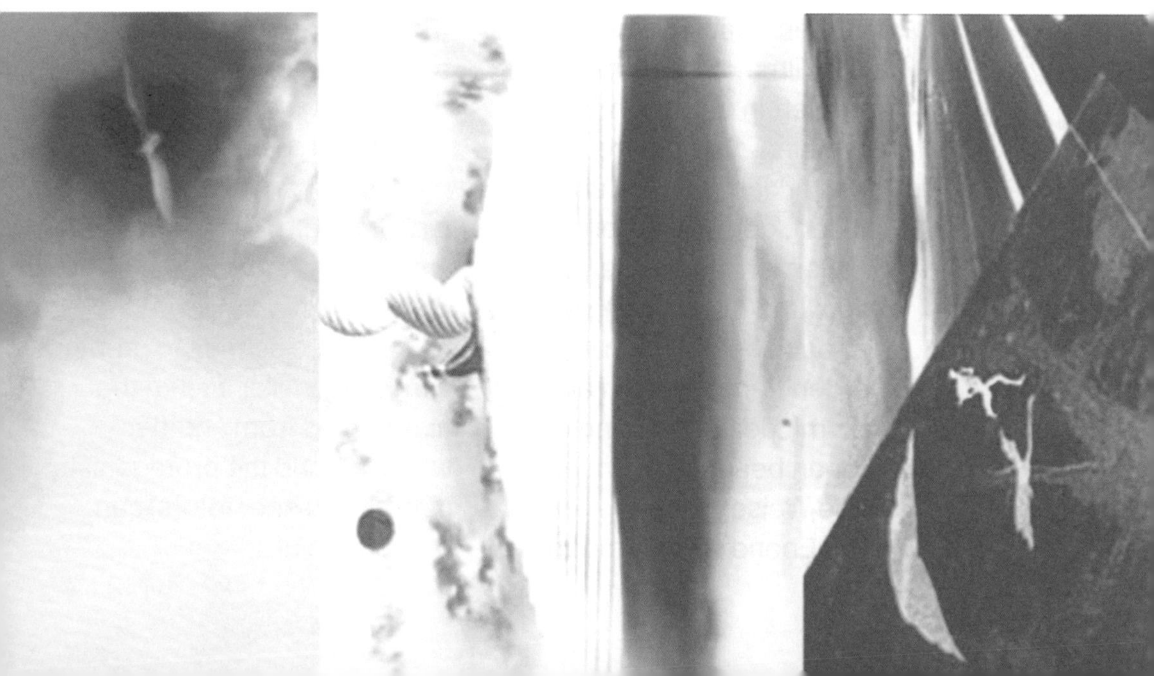

sogar elefantische Choreografien–mal flackrig, mal weichgeblendet; mal absurd, mal abstrus; mal blutig, mal knutschig; mal innovativ, mal exploitativ... Geführt von Morpheus tauchen wir dabei ein in ein Paralleluniversum der Kunst und Künstlichkeit, nicht zuletzt der unendlichen Freiheit. Denn hier zeigt sich, wild und ungezügelt, was sonst im Hintergrund lauert – so wie die Träume selbst, »die bei Nacht entstehen und am Tag vergehen« ...

tive, sometimes exploitative... Guided by Morpheus, we dive into a parallel universe of art and artifice, and last but not least, into endless freedom: because in these scenes, what is usually kept in the background is brought to the fore, on the screen – wildly and in your face, as do dreams themselves that »arise at nighttime and vanish by daytime«...

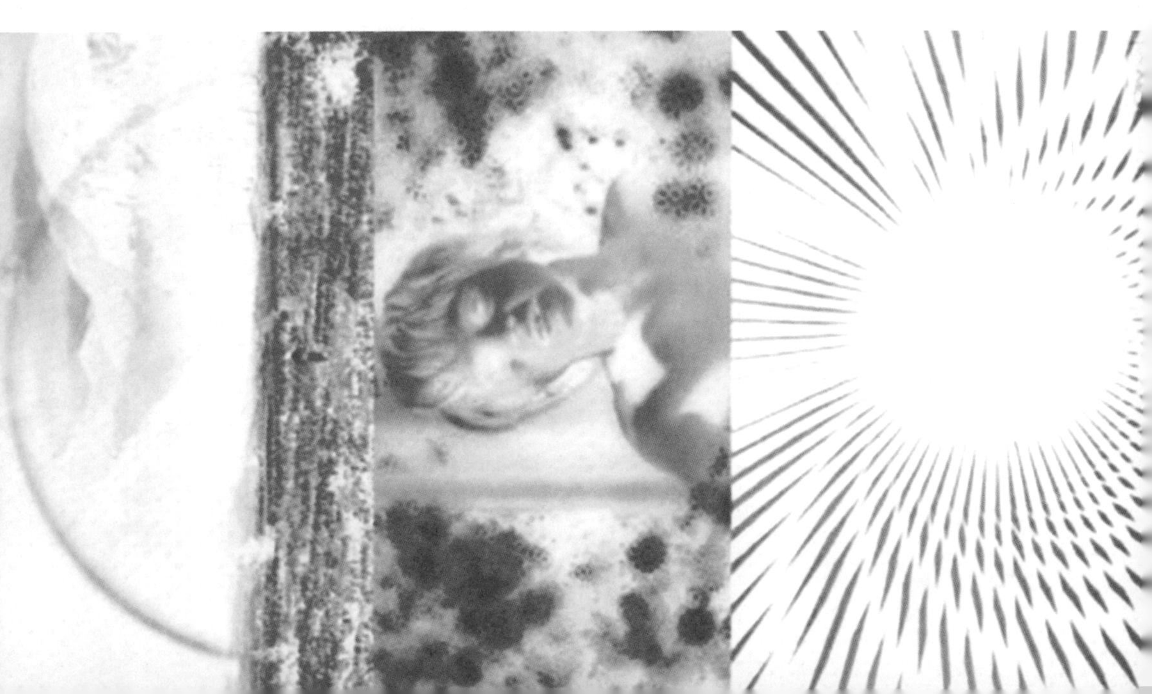

PHOBETOR

DE

Morpheus Bruder Phobetor verwandelt sich in den Träumen der Menschen in Erscheinungen wilder Tiere. Der nach ihm benannte zweite Teil der Trilogie der Traumgötterkonzerte rahmte das im »Dreamatory« stattfindende Symposium »Talk_about_Dreams« ein. Die Gesprächsrunde widmete sich natur- und kulturwissenschaftlichen Fragestellungen zur Funktion und Rolle des Träumens in Kunst und Gesellschaft. Sie eröffnete dem Publikum die Möglichkeit, die Wissenschaft und Kultur des Träumens aus unterschiedlichen disziplinären Perspektiven zu betrachten und mit führenden Wissenschaftler*innen dieses Feldes in Austausch zu treten. Moderiert wurde das Symposium von Agudio und Fingerhut.

EN

Within people's dreams, Morpheus's brother Phobetor takes on the shape of wild animals. The second part of the trilogy of the dreaming-god-concerts, which was named after him, gave a frame to the »Dreamatory« symposium »Talk_about_Dreams«. The roundtable focused on questions concerning the function and role of dreaming in art and society within the fields of natural and cultural science. The audience was given the opportunity to consider the science and culture of dreaming from different disciplinary perspectives and to interact with leading scientists in these fields. The symposium was moderated by Agudio and Fingerhut.

HARLEM

What happens to a dream deferred?

Does it dry up
like a raisin in the sun?
Or fester like a sore—
And then run?
Does it stink like rotten meat?
Or crust and sugar over—
like a syrupy sweet?

Maybe it just sags
like a heavy load.

Or does it explode?

Langston Hughes

DREAMER

I take my dreams
And make of them a bronze vase,
And a wide round fountain
With a beautiful statue in its center
And a song with a broken heart,
And I ask you:
Do you understand my dreams?
Sometimes you say you do
And sometimes you say you don't.
Either way
It doesn't matter.
I continue to dream.

Langston Hughes

Elena Agudio

»AM RANDE DES BEWUSSTSEINS. SIGHTSEEING IM REICH DER TRÄUME«

AT THE EDGE OF CONSCIOUSNESS. SIGHTSEEING IN THE REALM OF DREAMS

DE

Der Seiltänzer. Ein Bild. Eine Praxis. Nicht zuletzt eine Übung der guten Balance. Hinunterschauend, tief in Richtung der Dunkelheit und der Rätsel des eigenen Unbewusstseins, in dem Monster, Prinzessinnen und Drachen nach opulenten Festessen im Stillen tanzen, und hinaufblickend, in Richtung Tageslicht, wo die lichte Nachvollziehbarkeit von Fakten und Umständen liegt. Im ständigen Wechsel zwischen Schlaf und Wachsein, zwischen Ruhezustand und Bewegung sind wir Wesen, die das Gleichgewicht suchen im ständigen Hin und Her zwischen unserem realen Leben und der Welt unserer Träume. Eine Leistung, die die meisten von uns mit einer gewissen Lässigkeit und Leichtigkeit ausführen können: mit bewussten und unbewussten Angelegenheiten jonglierend,

EN

The tightrope walker. An image. A practice. An exercise of good balance, after all. Looking down, deep towards the darkness and the intricate puzzles of one's own unconscious, where monsters, princesses and dragons are dancing in silence after opulent banquets, and upwards, towards the light of the day, where the thin transparency of facts and circumstances lies. Constantly alternating between sleep and wakefulness, between dormancy and action, we are beings in equilibrium, performing the fluttering between our real lives and the realm of our dreams. A performance the majority of us can deliver with a certain nonchalance and facility: juggling conscious and unconscious matter, smuggling the memory of lived experiences and their symbolic content,

Erinnerungen gelebter Erfahrungen und deren symbolischen Gehalt von einem Ort zum anderen schmuggelnd – dies ist es eine der fundamentalen Tätigkeiten, die das menschliche Gehirn in der täglichen kognitiven Arbeit und Routine bewerkstelligt. Aber was passiert, wenn Mayas Schleier zerreisst und die dünne Membran, die die osmotische Beziehung zwischen der geträumten und der realen Welt regelt, löchrig wird?

Offenbar sind geträumte und reale Erfahrungen tatsächlich eng miteinander verbunden. Deshalb sollten sie nicht als zwei verschiedene, sondern als Hand in Hand gehende Welten verstanden werden, als Welt innerhalb einer anderen Welt.

Von Anbeginn an und über verschiedene Kulturkreise und Traditionen hinweg sind Träume bevorzugter Gegenstand von Künstler*innen, Dichter*innen, Denker*innen und Visionär*innen, Rebell*innen und Revolutionär*innen gewesen. Sie haben viel dazu beigetragen, die ihnen zugrundeliegenden Strukturen, Funktionen und ihren innersten Wesensgehalt zu verstehen.

is one of the fundamental activities the human brain is accomplishing in its daily cognitive labour and routine. But what happens if Maya's veil lacerates, and the thin membrane regulating the osmotic relation between the dreamt and the real world perforate? Apparently, the dreaming and waking experience are actually intimately entangled, hence they should not be imagined as two different worlds, but worlds that go hand in hand, a world within a world.

Since the beginning of time, across different cultures and traditions, dreams have been the privileged subject matter of artists and poets, thinkers and visionaries, rebels and revolutionaries. These people were advanced in the understanding of their structures, functions and most intimate substance.

In spite of this, the science of dreams and the neurology of dreams is still quite rocky and vague terrain. Not much is known about the secrecies of oneirology, about our hermetically sealed dreaming brains, and scientists so far are struggling to understand the content and purpose of dreams (well, this is sometimes the problem with scien-

Trotz alledem ist die Wissenschaft der Träume, die Neurologie der Träume, immer noch ein ziemlich wackliges und diffuses Terrain. Nur wenig ist bekannt über die Geheimnisse der Oneirologie, über unsere hermetisch abgeschlossenen, träumenden Gehirne. Wissenschaftler*innen haben sich bisher schwergetan, den Inhalt und Nutzen von Träumen zu verstehen (nun ja, das ist manchmal das Problem mit Wissenschaftler*innen, sie wollen für jedes Augenzwinkern einen Grund finden!), obgleich sie im Laufe der Menschheitsgeschichte schon immer Gegenstand des wissenschaftlichen, philosophischen und religiösen Interesses waren.

Wie allgemein bekannt, vertritt die Psychoanalyse die Ansicht, dass Träume Einblicke in verborgene Begierden und Gefühle gewähren. Andere wissenschaftliche Theorien argumentieren, dass Träume bei der Erinnerungsbildung und beim Finden von Problemlösungen helfen oder dass sie einfach ein Produkt willkürlicher Gehirnaktivität sind. Stephan LaBerge, der für seine Studien über Klarträume bekannt ist, betont, dass Träume teilweise dazu dienen, unbewusste Elemente

tists, willing to find a reason for every blink of an eye!), though they have been a topic of scientific, philosophical and religious interest throughout recorded history.

As is known, psychoanalysis suggests that dreams reveal insight into hidden desires and emotions. Other scientific theories propose that dreams assist in memory formation, problem solving, or argue that they simply are a product of random brain activities. Stephan LaBerge, renowned for his studies on lucid dreaming, suggests that dreams may function, in part, to recombine unconscious elements within consciousness on a temporary basis by a process he calls »mental recombination«.

A recent study at the University of Wisconsin Madison proved that dreams are not only occurring during rapid eye-movement (REM) sleep, a period of slumber involving fast brain activity similar to that when awake, but also during non-REM sleep.[1] In an interview with the Guardian, one of the authors of the study, Francesca Siclari, declares: »It seemed a mystery that you can have both dreaming and the absence

für eine bestimmte Zeit ins Bewusstsein zu holen. Diesen Prozess nennt er »mental recombination« (mentale Rekombination).

Eine 2017 an der University of Wisconsin-Madison durchgeführte Studie zeigte, dass Träume nicht nur während des REM-Schlafs, sondern auch während des Non-REM-Schlafs entstehen.[1] In einem Interview mit The Guardian erklärt eine der Autor*innen der Studie, Francesca Siclari: »Es erschien wie ein Rätsel, dass man in diesen zwei verschiedenen Phasen sowohl träumen also auch nicht träumen kann.« Die Studie »beweist die Tatsache, dass Träumen tatsächlich eine Erfahrung ist, die während des Schlafes stattfindet. Viele Wissenschaftlicher gehen bis heute davon aus, dass es etwas ist, dass man erfindet, wenn man wach wird«, so Siclari. »Möglicherweise ist das schlafende Gehirn dem wachen Gehirn viel ähnlicher als bisher vorstellbar, da es teilweise auf dieselben Bereiche für die gleiche Art von Erfahrung zurückgreift.«[2]

In jedem Fall gilt, wie es bereits Thomas Metzinger vor einigen Jahren und noch vor Aufkommen der aktuel-

of dreaming in these two different types of stages.« The study is »a proof for the fact that dreaming really is an experience that occurs during sleep, because many researchers up until now have suggested that it is just something you invent when you wake up.« »Maybe the dreaming brain and the waking brain are much more similar than one imagined because they partially recruit the same areas for the same type of experiences.«[2]

In any case, as Thomas Metzinger has already mentioned some years ago, before the flourishing of contemporary studies on dreams: »Today, the phenomenon of dreaming has not only become one of the most interesting objects of study at the interface between philosophy of mind and empirical research programmes, but a genuine research tool in itself. One hope is to use dreams as an instrument that guides researchers to a deeper understanding of consciousness, self-consciousness, and subjectivity.«[3]

With the symposium »At the Edge of Consciousness. Sightseeing in the Realm of Dreams«, a discursive event

1 Francesca Siclari, Benjamin Baird, Lampros Perogamvros, Giulio Bernardi, Joshua J. LaRocque, Brady Riedner, Melanie Boly, Bradley R Postle und Giulio Tononi, The Neural Correlates of Dreaming, in: Nature Neuroscience 20, 2017, S. 872–878, (retrieved 22.01.2017) https://doi.org/doi:10.1038/nn.4545.

2 Nicola Davis, Scientists Identify Parts of Brain Involved in Dreaming, in: The Guardian 10.4.2017, (retrieved 22.01.2017) https://www.theguardian.com/science/2017/apr/10/scientists-identify-parts-of-brain-involved-in-dreaming.

len Diskussion formuliert hat: »Das Phänomen des Träumens ist nicht nur zu einem der interessantesten Untersuchungsgegenstände an der Schnittstelle zwischen Geistesphilosophie und empirischer Forschung, sondern zu einem originären Forschungsinstrument an sich geworden. Eine Hoffnung besteht darin, Träume als Mittel zu verwenden, um zu einem tieferen Verständnis des Bewusstseins, des Selbstbewusstseins und der Subjektivität zu gelangen.«[3]

Das Symposium »At the Edge of Consciousness. Sightseeing in the Realm of Dreams« war eine diskursive Veranstaltung, die Joerg Fingerhut und ich im Rahmen von Viron Erol Verts Soloausstellung in der Galerie Wedding »The Name of Shades of Paranoia, Called Different Forms of Silence« für die »Association of Neuroesthetics« (AoN) kuratiert haben. Wir sahen es als Möglichkeit, die wissenschaftliche und kulturelle Dimension der Träume aus der Perspektive unterschiedlicher Disziplinen zu untersuchen, indem wir einige führende Wissenschaftler*innen aus diesem Bereich baten, sich mit Verts Werk auseinanderzusetzen und sich mit be-

myself and Joerg Fingerhut curated for »Association of Neuroesthetics« (AoN) in the framework of Viron Erol Vert's solo show at Galerie Wedding »The Name of Shades of Paranoia, Called Different Forms of Silence«, we took the opportunity to explore the science and culture of dreams from different disciplinary perspectives, asking some leading scientists in the field to engage with Vert's work and addressing them with some conundrums. How do dreams materialise in the brain and how do dreams relate to other large scale brain activities to motor engagement and attention? In what ways could dreams be manipulated or influenced? Are they biologically determined or culturally construed and different across cultures? What is the relation of dreams and art and aesthetic experiences? How do the metaphorical language of dream symbols and the one of artistic visions relate to each other? Are dreams acts of political imaginations?

The »Association of Neuroesthetics« (AoN) is a Berlin based platform for neuroscience and art, promoting projects, interdisciplinary research and knowledge

3 Thomas Metzinger, Why Are Dreams Interesting for Philosophers? The Example of Minimal Phenomenal Selfhood, Plus an Agenda for Future Research, in: Frontiers in Psychology 4, 2013, Art. 746, retrieved (22.02.2017) https://doi.org/10.3389/fpsyg.2013.00746.

stimmten Fragestellungen zu befassen: Wie materialisieren sich Träume im Gehirn und in welcher Beziehung stehen sie zu anderen, großen Gehirnaktivitäten, die Aufträge erteilen und Aufmerksamkeit ermöglichen? Auf welche Weise können Träume manipuliert oder beeinflusst werden? Sind sie biologisch bestimmt oder kulturell konstruiert und je nach Kulturkreis verschieden? Wie ist der Zusammenhang zwischen Träumen, Kunst und ästhetischer Erfahrung? Gibt es eine Verbindung zwischen der metaphorischen Sprache der Traumsymbole und derjenigen künstlerischer Visionen? Sind Träume Akte politischer Vorstellungen?

Die »Association of Neuroesthetics« (AoN) ist eine Plattform für Neurowissenschaften und Kunst in Berlin, die in Zusammenarbeit mit der Charité – Universitätsmedizin und der School of Mind and Brain der Humboldt Universität Projekte interdisziplinäre Forschungsvorhaben und den Wissensaustausch zwischen Kunst und Kognitionswissenschaft fördert.

exchange between art and cognitive sciences, in collaboration with the Medical University of Charité and The School of Mind and Brain of the Humboldt University.

Coloured sagittal MRI scans of the human brain. Changes in brain activity offer clues to what the dream is about.
Photo: Simon Frazer/SPL/Getty Images

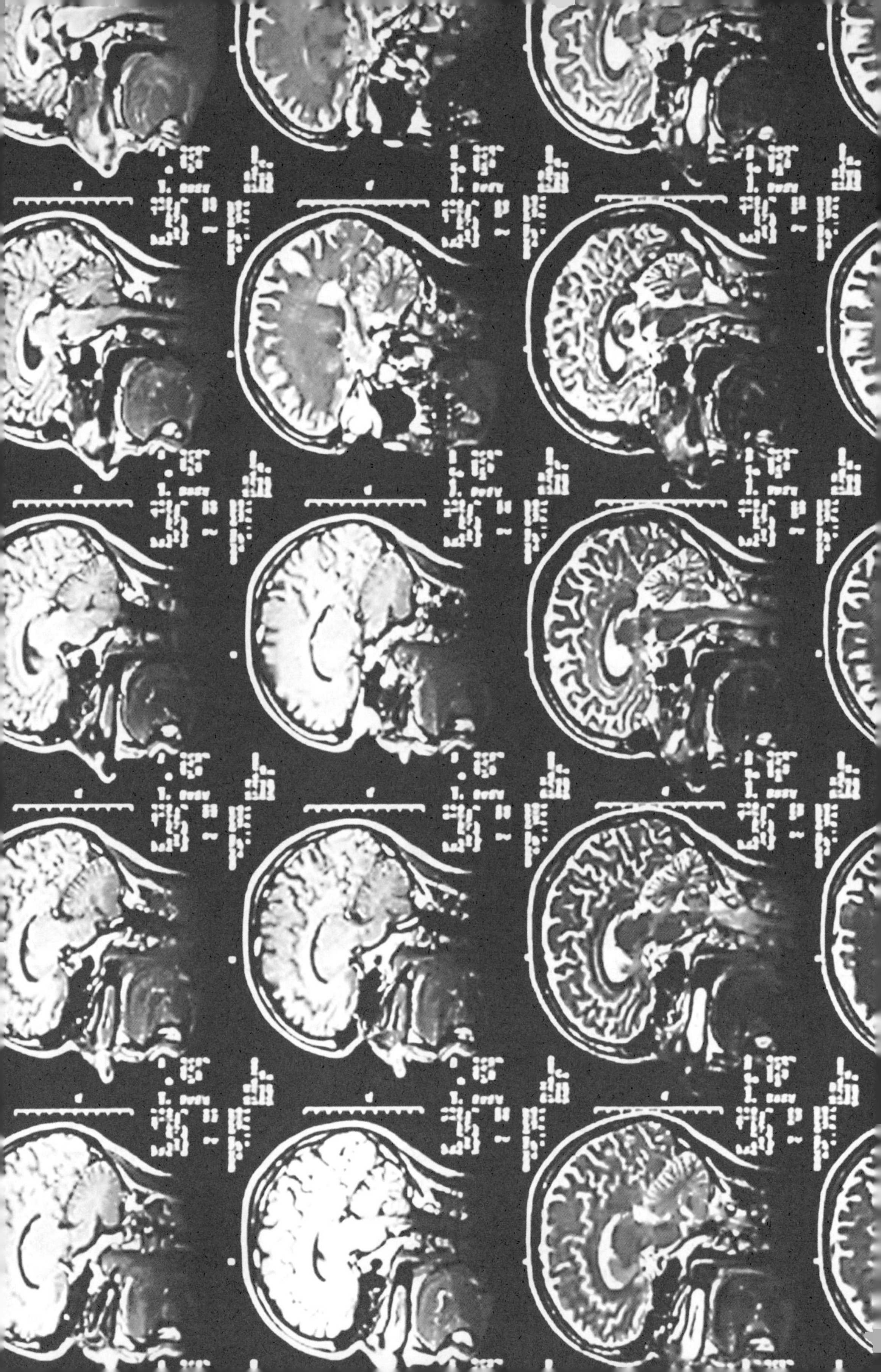

Holger Brohm

EINE SEHR KURZE EINFÜHRUNG IN DIE KULTURGESCHICHTE DES TRÄUMENS

A VERY SHORT INTRODUCTION TO THE CULTURAL HISTORY OF DREAMING

DE

Nicht die Menschen allein träumen, auch Tiere verfügen über diese Fähigkeit. Aber nur die Menschen erzählen ihre Traumwahrnehmungen, schreiben sie auf und bewahren sie in ihrer Erinnerung. Sie geben den nächtlichen Bildern Bedeutungen, um die Welt zu verstehen und ihre Position in der Welt zu bestimmen. Menschliche Träume sind somit als kulturelles Phänomen anzusehen, das in eine Vielzahl von Prozessen eingebettet ist. Das schließt die unmittelbaren Praktiken des Umgangs mit den Träumen, ebenso wie Konzepte des Körpers oder weiterreichende philosophische Entwürfe des Selbst der Träumenden ein. Zwar haben Menschen immer geträumt, doch haben sich ihre Vorstellungen davon, was ein Traum ist, gewandelt. Auf die westliche Welt bezogen, lassen sich die Veränderungen vor allem

EN

It is not only humans who dream, animals have this ability, too. Though it is only humans who share with others their perception of dreaming, who note them down and preserve them in memory. They give this nocturnal imagery meaning in order to understand the world and determine their position within it. Human dreams must thus be viewed as cultural phenomena embedded in a multitude of processes. This includes the direct practices of the handling of dreams; equally, concepts of the body or extensive philosophical designs of the Self of the dreaming. Humans have always dreamed, but the idea of what constitutes a dream has diversified. With the Western world, the changes can be observed primarily through the transformation of cultural knowledge pertaining

im Wandel des kulturellen Wissens über die Herkunft der Träume und ihre Bedeutungen beobachten. So wurden in der Antike Träume als göttlichen Ursprungs verstanden, nicht alle Träume verfügten aber über die gleiche Aussagekraft. So heißt es in Homers Odyssee: »Es gibt zwei Pforten für die flüchtigen Träume: eine aus Horn, die andere aus Elfenbein. Die durch das polierte Elfenbein kommen, trügen uns und bringen leere Worte; und die durch das geglättete Horn gehen, verkünden den Sterblichen Dinge, die wirklich wahr werden.« In unserer Traumkultur hat sich die Faszination für das Spektakel der nächtlichen Bilder erhalten, jedoch ging im Verlauf der Jahrhunderte der Glaube an die göttliche Herkunft und an das Visionäre verloren, stattdessen werden die Träume mit der individuellen Geschichte der Träumenden verbunden und als Speicher der Erinnerungen verstanden. Kürzt man die lange Geschichte ab, so erweist sich der Traum als schwer greifbar, zwischen dem Heiligen und dem Profanen, zwischen Zukunft und Vergangenheit, zwischen dem Somatischen und dem Semiotischen wandelnd. Die Geschichte des Traums ist nicht abgeschlossen, sie ist stets offen für neue Entwicklungen.

to the origin of dreams and their meanings. In ancient times, dreams were understood as the divine origin, though not all dreams had equal significance. As the saying in Homer's Odyssey goes: »There are two gates through which these unsubstantial fancies proceed; the one is of horn, and the other ivory. Those that come through the gate of ivory are fatuous, but those from the gate of horn mean something to those that see them.« In our dream culture, the fascination for the spectacle of nocturnal imagery has been maintained; however, faith in the divine origin and in visionaries has been lost over the centuries. Instead, dreams became connected to the individual history of the dreamers and are understood as a storage of memories. If the longer story is shortened, the dream proves itself to be barely graspable – shifting between the divine and the profane, between future and past, between the somatic and the semiotic. The history of the dream has not been concluded. It is always open to new developments.

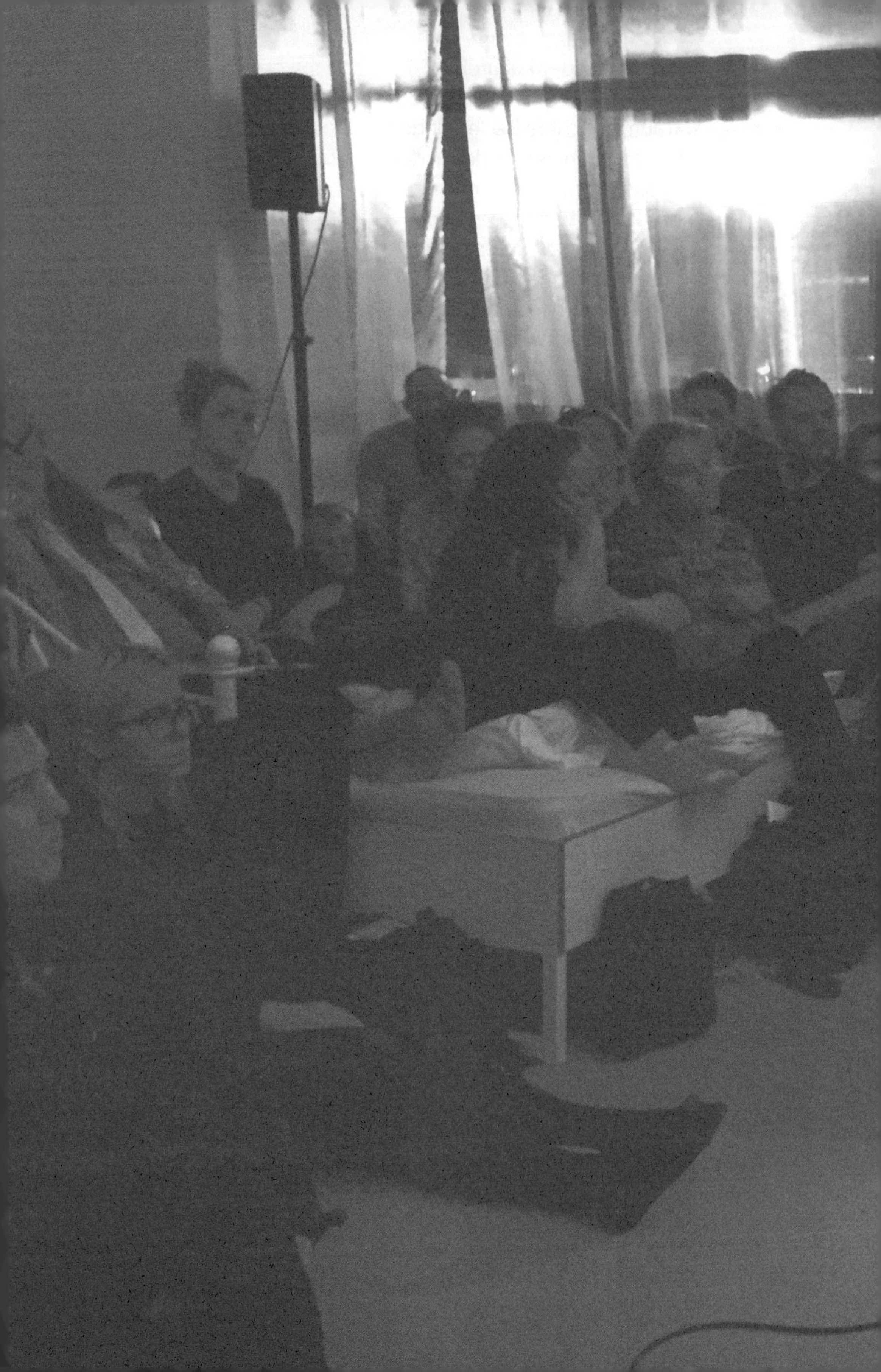

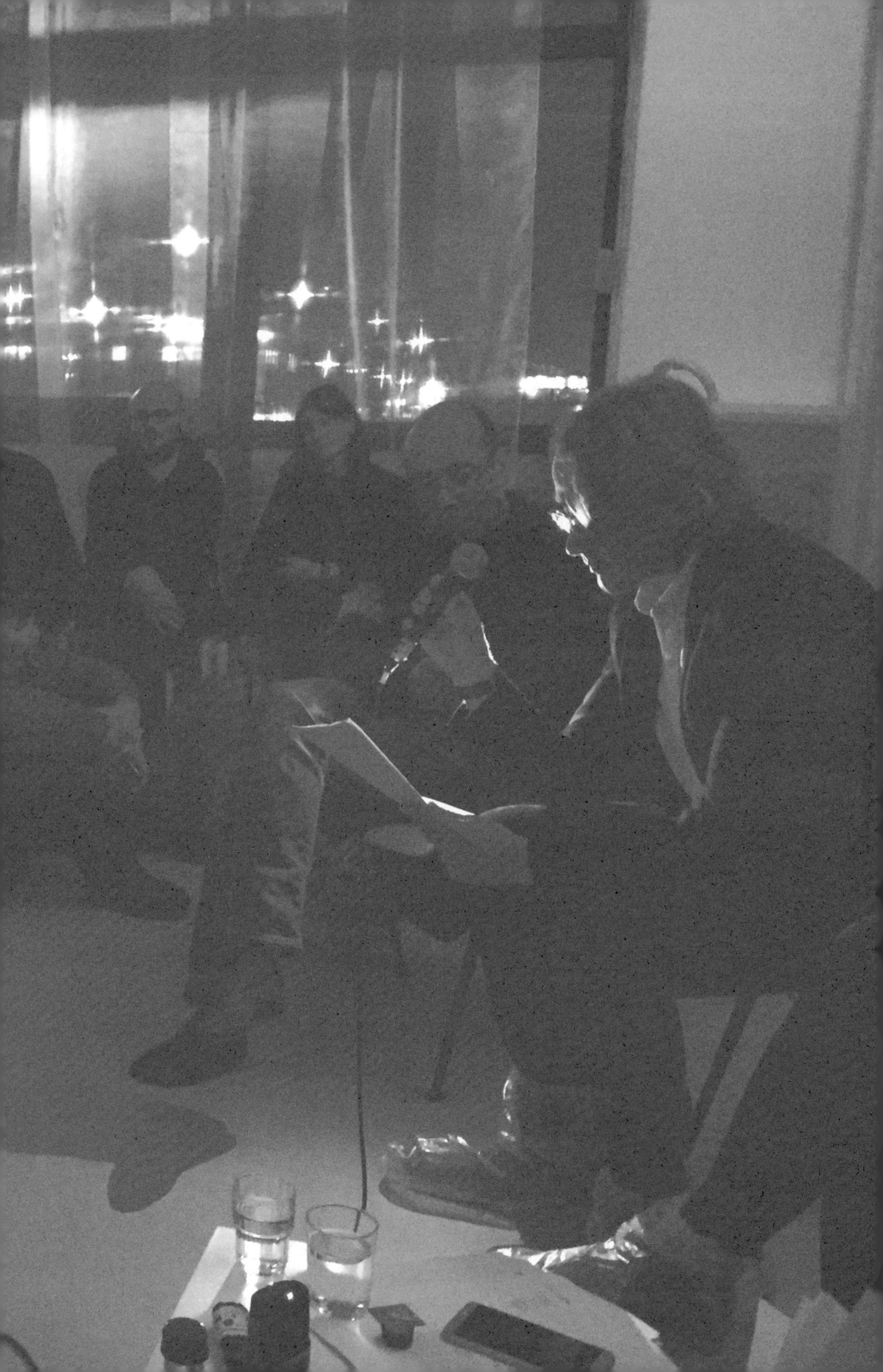

Joerg Fingerhut

KUNST ALS VON AUSSEN GELEITETER TRAUM

ART AS EXTERNALLY-GUIDED DREAMING

DE

Weder die mäandernden Verästelungen unserer Phantasie und Träume noch die öffentliche Teilbarkeit von Erfahrungen – beides zentrale Elemente von Viron Erol Verts Arbeit »The Name of Shades of Paranoia, Called Different Forms of Silence« – scheinen zunächst in das Muster der Neuroästhetik zu passen. Dieses beruht vor allem auf Stimulus (Präsentation eines Kunstwerkes) => Reaktion (Messung neuronaler Aktivität). Dennoch gibt es Arbeiten, die eine erstaunliche Verbindung von Traum und Kunst, von Innenwelt und Auseinandersetzung mit einem Kunstwerk nachweisen konnten. So hat ein Forscher*innenteam um den Neurowissenschaftler Ed Vessel seine Proband*innen gebeten, verschiedenste visuelle Kunstwerke daraufhin zu betrachten, ob sie diese zur Anschaffung für ein Museum empfehlen würden.

EN

Neither the meandering ramifications of our fantasies and dreams, nor the public sharing of such experiences – both central elements of Viron Erol Vert's work »The Name of Shades of Paranoia, Called Different Forms of Silence« – seem to be assessable through the method of neuroesthetics. Such a method is still largely based on stimulus (presentation of reproductions of artworks) and response (measurements of neurological activity) and many studies focus on perceptual processes and simple preference ratings of the participants. Nevertheless, there are works in this field that demonstrate a rather staggering connection between dreaming and art, between our deepest inner processes and our engagement with artworks.

For instance, a team of researchers working with neu-

Die Wertung ging von 1 bis 4 und die Teilnehmer*innen sollten ihre Bewertung unter anderem darauf basieren, wie bewegend sie die Kunstwerke fanden. Während der Betrachtung der Kunstwerke wurde die Hirnaktivität der Teilnehmer*innen im MRT-Scanner gemessen. Die Forscher*innen fanden ein überraschendes neuronales Muster: Insbesondere im vorderen Bereich des Gehirns zeigte ein Netzwerk von kortikalen Arealen und im Thalamus eine verstärkte Aktivität, allerdings nur für die Kunstwerke, die als besonders bewegend (also mit »4«) eingestuft wurden. Dieses Netzwerk ist als das »Default Mode Network« (DMN) bekannt.

Zwei Dinge erscheinen hier besonders bemerkenswert. Erstens bestand keinerlei Einigkeit der Betrachter*innen darüber, welche Bilder die höchsten Ratings erhielten: Dies scheint eine zutiefst individuelle Einschätzung aller Betrachter*innen zu sein. Zweitens ist eine Aktivierung des DMN vor dieser Studie nie in Verbindung mit einem zugleich starken visuellen Engagement gefunden worden, die zeitgleich im visuellen Verarbeitungspfad der

roscientist Ed Vessel asked its subjects to look at visual artworks of various styles to determine whether they would be recommendable as acquisitions for a museum. They had to rate them from 1–4 (1 being the lowest, 4 the highest rating), based, among other factors, on how moving they found the artworks to be. During the examination of the artworks the brain activity of the participants was measured using an MRI scanner. The researchers discovered a surprising neuronal pattern, particularly in the anterior region of the brain and in a network spanning cortical areas and the thalamus. In these regions they found an increased activity, but only for those artworks which were catagorised as »particularly moving« (i.e. that received a 4 rating). This network is known as the »Default Mode Network« (DMN).

Two things seem particularly remarkable here: first, there was no consensus among the viewers as to which images received the highest ratings – this seemed to be subject to the highly personal assessment of the individual viewer. Secondly, activation of the DMN prior to this study was never connected to a simulta-

Proband*innen nachgewiesen wurde. Eine bekannte Funktion des DMN ist es nämlich, Tagträume zu ermöglichen, und es ist zum Beispiel auch aktiv, wenn wir über uns selbst reflektieren. Und hier schien zu gelten: Entweder verliert man sich in sich selbst, oder man verfolgt eine Aufgabe, die unsere Sinne mit einschließt.

Eine spekulative Folgerung aus dem beschriebenen Experiment ist, dass Kunst genau hier eine Brücke zu schlagen vermag. Sie ist sinnliches Engagement, das uns auf uns selbst zurückwirft. Sie kann in ihrer Betrachtung, im starken sensorischen Erleben, uns gleichzeitig zu einer Re-evaluation unserer selbst auffordern. Kunst, wenn sie erfolgreich ist, ist von außen geleitete Träumerei.

neous intense visual engagement. A known function of DMN is to enable daydreams; it is also active when we self-reflect. Yet in such instances either one loses oneself, or one pursues a task in which one's senses are directed outward to the world. One normally does not do both. Yet Vessel and colleagues found just this very peculiar combination: highly rated artworks activated a network that underlies our daydreams and they also perceptually engaged the viewers more intensely. This was indicated by a stronger neuronal activity in ventral visual pathways of the subjects for the artworks that they rated higher.

A speculative conclusion from the described experiment: it is precisely here that art can build a bridge. Sensory engagement with art thrusts us back against ourselves. By being captured by an artwork, by having intense aesthetic experiences, we are also prompted to re-evaluate ourselves. Art, if successful, is exteroceptively driven self-evaluation, it is a reverie guided from the outside.

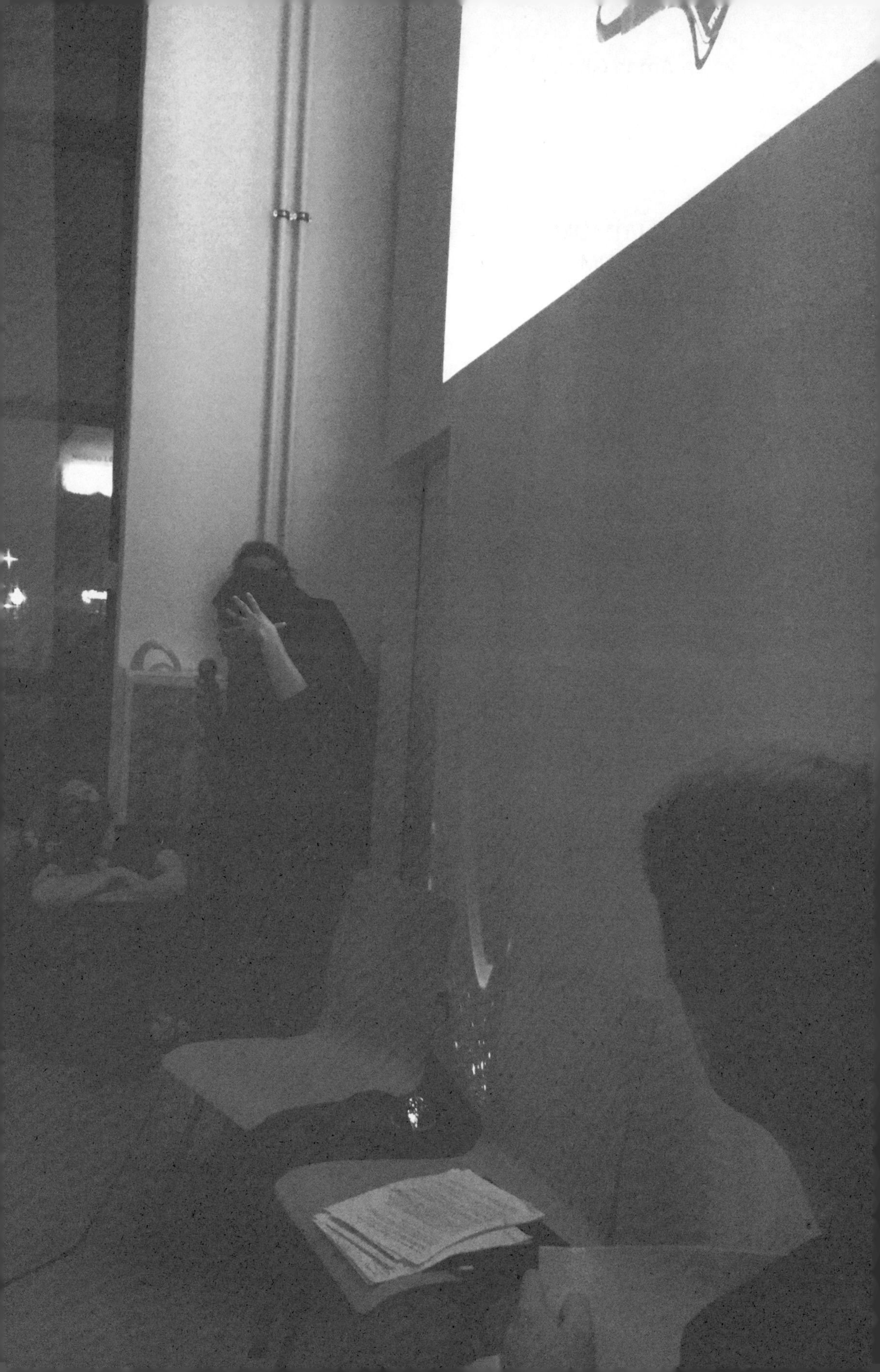

Amna Ghani

ERSCHAFFE EINEN TRAUM ODER EINEN ALBTRAUM MIT DEINEM GEHIRN!

CREATE A DREAM OR A NIGHTMARE WITH YOUR BRAIN!

DE

»My Virtual Dream (MVD)« ist eine immersive multimediale Umgebung. Zwischen Wissenschaft, Kunst und Musik ist MVD ein Unterhaltungs- und Lernprozess über das Gehirn, Gesundheit und Fitness. Bei der Performance von MVD sind die Performer*innen nichts anderes als die Gehirnströme der Besucher*innen. Mittels ihrer Gehirnströme wird eine breite Palette von Visuellem, Klang und Musik in Echtzeit produziert. Entwickelt von einem unglaublich talentierten Team aus Künstler*innen, Musiker*innen, Programmierer*innen, Wissenschaftler*innen und Ingenieur*innen erschafft MVD eine Traumkulisse in Abhängigkeit vom Traum der Person. Ist die Person eher entspannt, so ist die Traumlandschaft angenehm,

EN

»My Virtual Dream (MVD)« is an immersive multimedia environment. At the intersection of science, art and music, MVD is an entertainment and learning experience about brain health and fitness. In the show of MVD, performers are no one else but the audience's own brain waves. Using your brain waves, you co-create a vast array of visual, sound and music all projected in real-time live. Built by an incredibly talented team of artists, musicians, programmers, scientists and engineers, MVD creates a dream scene dependent on the dreamer's brain. If the person is more relaxed, the dreamscape becomes more pleasant, while focusing can create more dramatic dreams. Each dreamer has his own music layer, the

For more information please visit the virtual dream website www.myvirtualdream.net

während eine angespannte Person dramatische Träume erzeugt. Jede*r Träumende hat seine*ihre eigene Musikebene, das Volumen der Musikebene für jede*n Träumende*n wird durch den entspannten und fokussierten Zustand der Person gesteuert. MVD ist eine Initiative, um dem allgemeinen Publikum einen genaueren Blick in das Gehirn und seine Funktionsweise in einer kollektiven und künstlerischen Umgebung zu bieten. MVD findet jedes Jahr während der Langen Nacht der Wissenschaften an der Charité – Universitätsmedizin Berlin statt.

volume of the music layer for each dreamer is controlled by the relaxed and focused state of a dreamer. MVD is an initiative to provide the general audience with a closer look into their brain and its functioning in a more collective and artistic environment. MVD takes place every year during the long night of sciences in Charité – Universitätsmedizin Berlin.

Pascal Grosse

IKONOGRAFISCHE REPRÄSENTATIONEN VON RÄUMEN DES TRAUMES – VERGANGENHEIT UND GEGENWART

ICONOGRAPHIC REPRESENTATION OF DREAMS AND SPACES – PAST AND PRESENT

DE

Sowohl in der Gegenwart als auch in der Vergangenheit gab es zahlreiche ikonografische Darstellungen von Schlaf und Traum. Demzufolge war die Biologie von Schlaf und Traum bisher immer in eine historisch veränderbare kulturelle Matrix eingebettet. Schlaf, als eine Zeit der Erholung, ein Rückzug aus der realen Welt, und als der (jüngere) Bruder des Todes, ist wie der Traum eine Sphäre unterdrückter Wünsche, des (fast) Unerreichbaren und des nächtlichen kognitiven Chaos kultureller Konstruktionen. All das gibt Schlafen und Träumen eine ganz andere Bedeutung und führt wiederum zu einem Bedeutungsverlust. Dazu gehört auch die Idee des »Labors« als moderne Messstation von Schlaf und Traum, in der sich die subjektive Realität der eigenen

EN

Both present and past have presented numerous iconographic representations of sleep and dream. Thus, the biology of sleep and dream has until now always been embedded within a historically changeable cultural matrix. Sleep, as a time to recover, a withdrawal from the real world, and as death's (younger) brother, are equal to the dream as a sphere of suppressed desires, to the (almost) unattainable, and the nocturnal cognitive chaos of cultural constructions, all of which give sleeping and dreaming quite different meaning and in turn bring about a loss of meaningfulness. Contained within this is the idea of the »laboratory« as a modern measuring station of sleep and dream which confronts the subjective reality of one's own ex-

Erfahrungen und die scheinbar objektive Erörterung zahlreicher Messdaten als »wahre Realität« begegnen. Allerdings ist eben auch das Schlaflabor nur ein Teil der Genealogie seiner ikonografische Vorgänger wie Michelangelo (»Il Sogno«, um 1533) und Johann Heinrich Füssli (»Nachtmahr«, um 1781) zu Francisco de Goya (»El Sueño de la Razón Produce Monstruos«, ca. 1798) und Pierre Narcisse Guérin (»Morphée et Iris«, 1811) an Jean-Jacques Grandville (»Premier Rêve«, 1847) und Frida Kahlo (»El Sueño«, 1940). Wurden in der Ikonografie des 19. Jahrhunderts Signaturen wie der Alb verwendet, um Schlafen und Träumen sichtbar und erkennbar zu machen, so hat die Ikonografie seit dem 19. Jahrhundert versucht, die Subjektivität des Schlafens und Träumens darzustellen — nämlich die Auflösung von Raum und Zeit während der Schlafphasen. In dieser Hinsicht ist das Schlaflabor eine Hybride: Es ist eine Signatur zum Schlafen und Träumen— es zeigt seinen einzigen Zweck, das Maß des Schlafes zu sein; der Vergleich der ikonografischen Vorgänger des Schlaflabors deutet darauf hin, dass die Technik die individuelle sub-

perience with a seemingly objective finding of numerous measured data as »true reality«. Nevertheless, the sleep laboratory, too, is merely part of the genealogy of its iconographic predecessors such as Michelangelo (»Il Sogno«, ca. 1533) and Johann Heinrich Füssli (»Nachtmahr« ca. 1781) to Francisco Goya (»El Sueño de la Razón Produce Monstruos«, ca. 1798) and Pierre Narcisse Guérin (»Morphée et Iris«, 1811) to Jean-Jacques Grandville (Premier rêve, 1847) and Frida Kahlo (»El Sueño«, 1940). If, in pre-19th century iconography, signatures were used such as the incubus (to render sleeping and dreaming visibly recognisable, then ever since the 19th century, iconography has attempted to depict the subjectivity of the sleeping and dreaming—namely the dissolution of space and time during periods of sleep. In this respect, the sleep laboratory is a hybrid: it is a signature for sleeping and dreaming — showing its sole purpose to be the measurement of sleep; simultaneously, the iconography of the sleep laboratory suggests that technology makes the individually subjective experience objectively reproducible. This has been proven to be false.

jektive Erfahrung objektiv reproduzierbar macht. Dies hat sich als falsch erwiesen. Im Schlaflabor werden lediglich Hirnströme und andere biologische Signale gemessen, nicht Inhalte von Gedanken und Empfindungsarten.

In the sleep laboratory, it is merely brain currents and other biological signals that are measured, not content of thought and types of sensations.

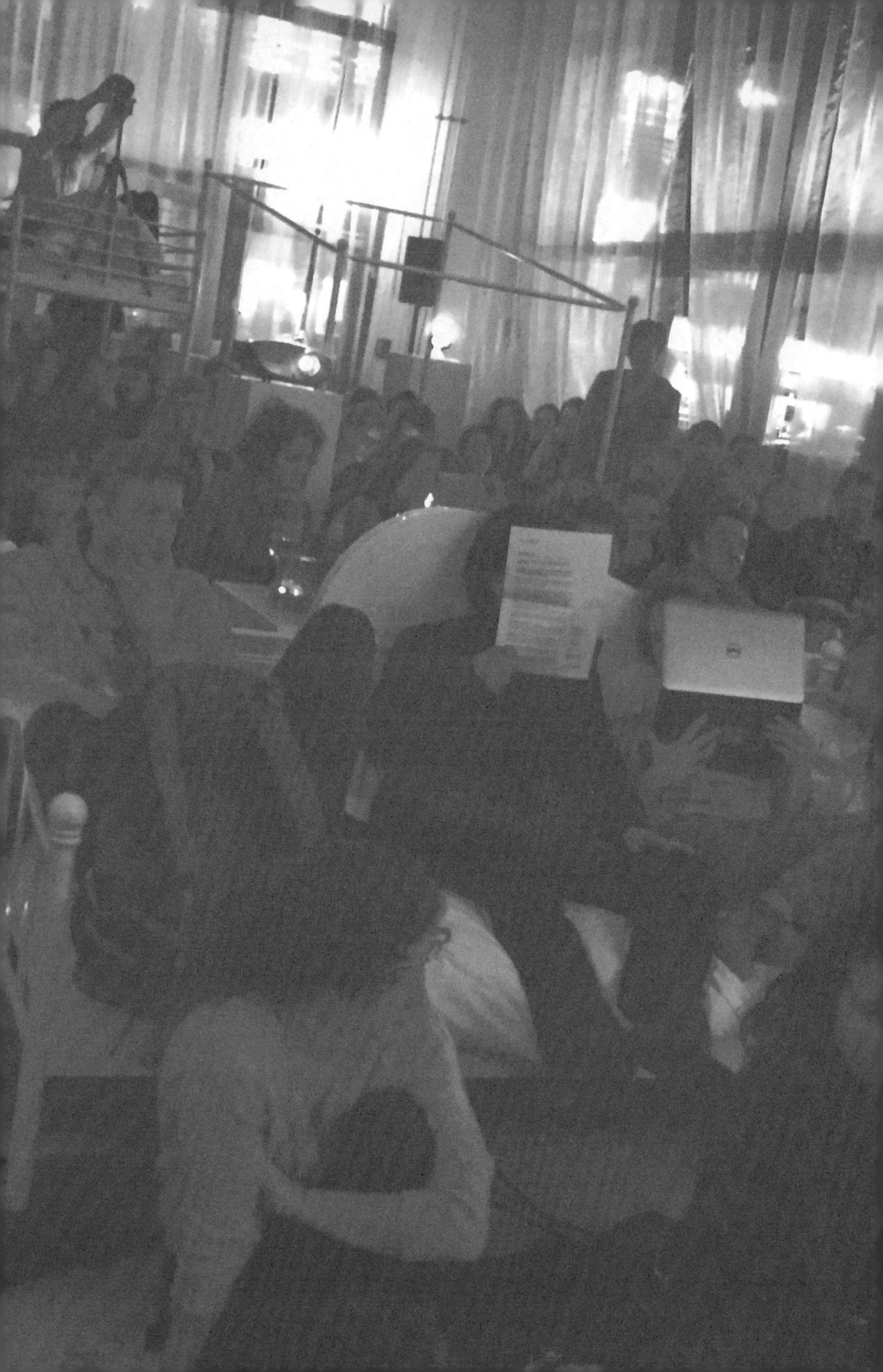

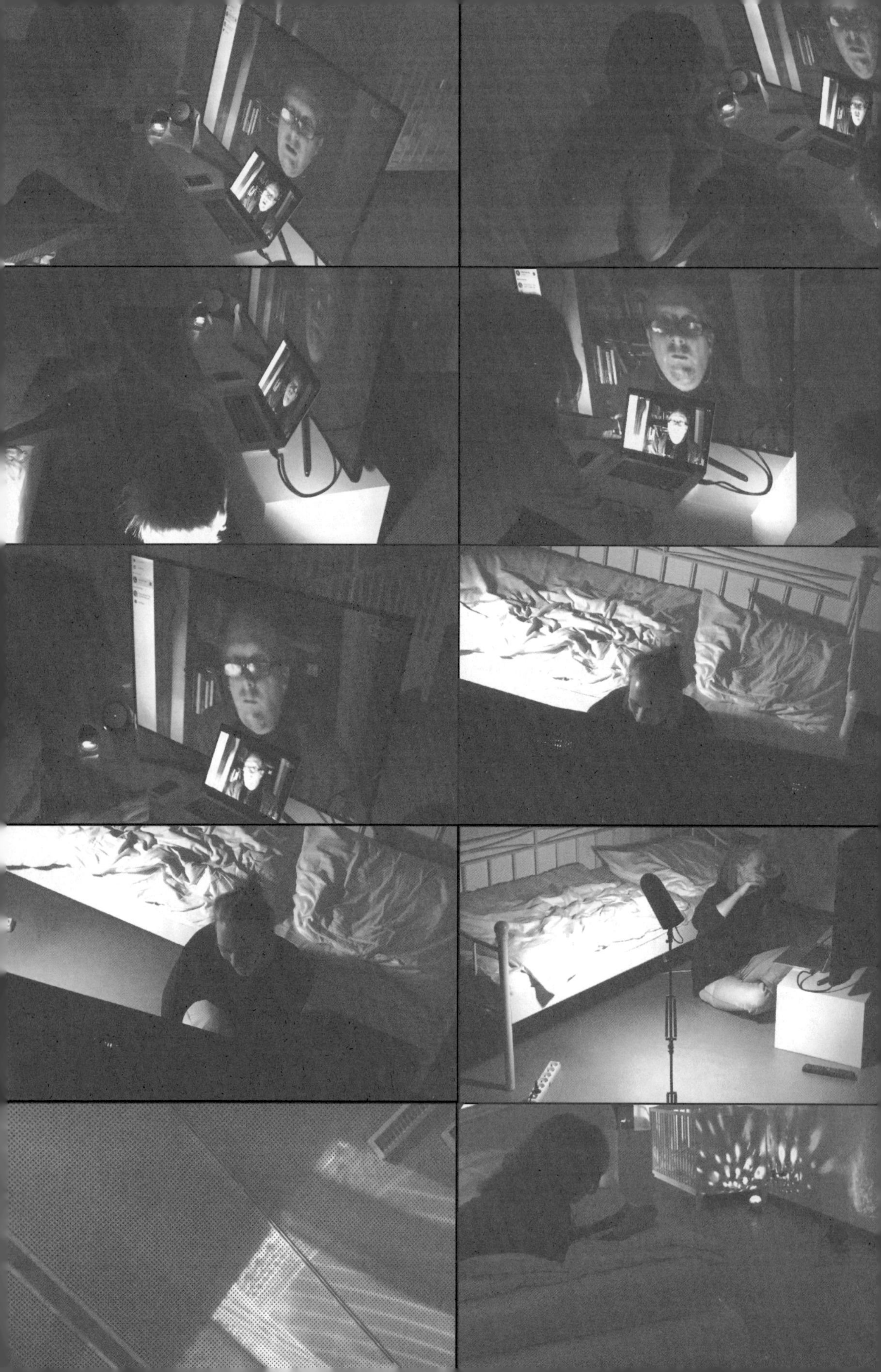

ONEIROI-CRITICS-SESSION

DE

Der renommierte Traumspezialist Michael Mollura wurde via Skype-Call live aus Beverly Hills, Kalifornien, ins »Dreamatory« der Galerie Wedding geschaltet. In etwa 15-minütigen Gesprächen konnten die Teilnehmer*innen der Sitzung Mollura ihre Träume schildern, woraufhin der Experte diese analysierte und deutete.

EN

Renowned dream specialist Michael Mollura was transmitted live to the »Dreamatory« at Galerie Wedding via Skype from Beverly Hills, California. Participants were invited to describe their dreams within a 15 minute session with Mollura in order to let them be analysed and interpreted by the specialist.

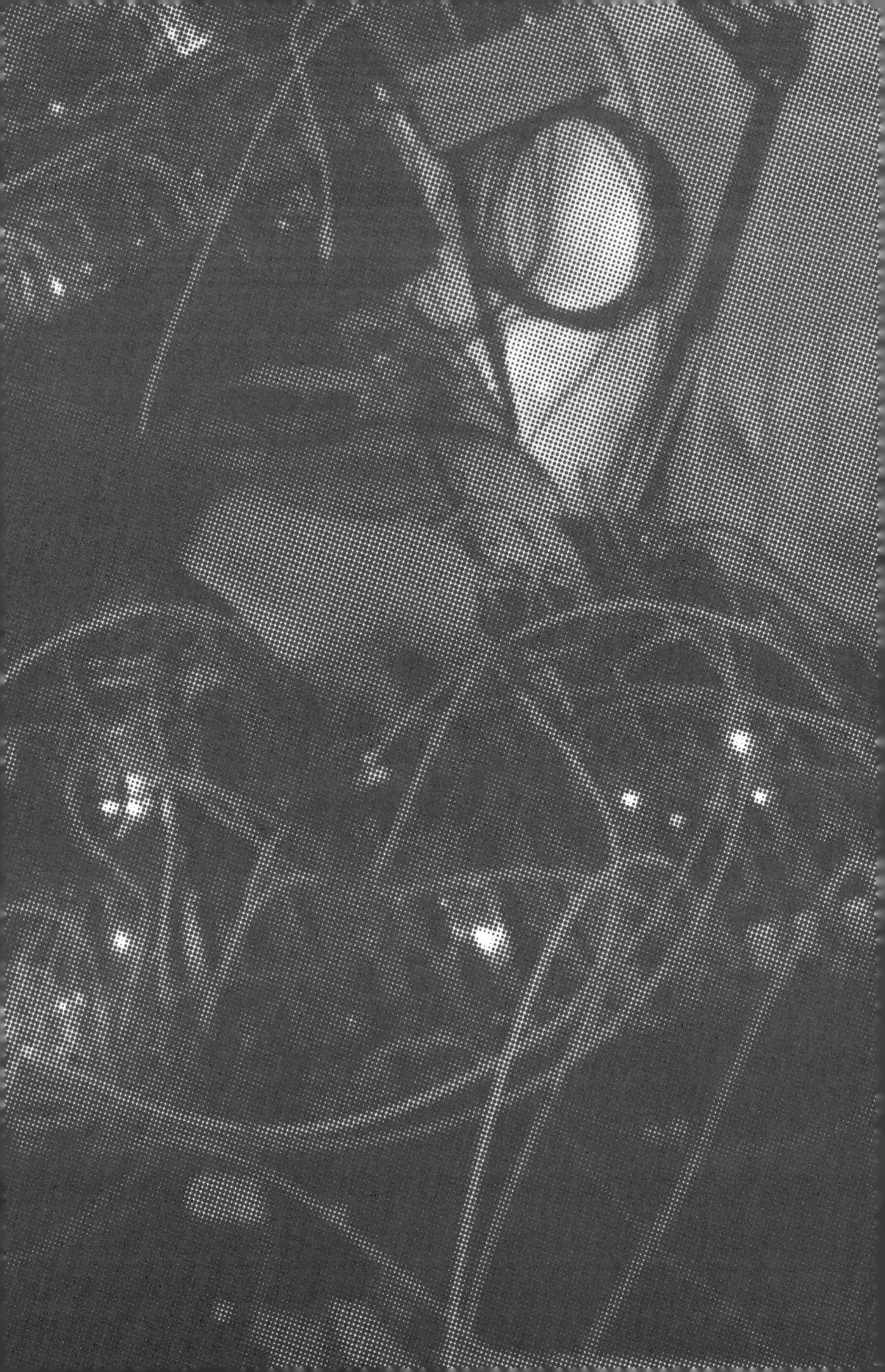

PHANTASOS

DE

Die Live-Performance, mit der »Driftmachine« ihre Trilogie abschloss, widmete sich dem Oneiros Phantasos, dem in der Ausgestaltung der Träume der Bereich der leblosen Gegenstände und der Naturgewalten unterliegt. Viron Erol Vert reagierte in seiner nach Einbruch der Dunkelheit abgehaltenen Live-Drawing-Performance, die an die Galeriewände projiziert nachvollzogen werden konnte, nicht nur auf die sich im »Dreamatory« entfaltende Soundcollage. Im beständigen Akt des Zeichnens sich zunehmend überlagernder Linien mit variierendem Duktus ausgeführt lag auch der Versuch, eine Ebene der Ratio zu transzendieren und sich einer Logik des Traumes anzunähern, in welcher der Geist frei und sprunghaft von einem Gedanken zum nächsten zieht.

EN

The last live performance by »Driftmachine« that completed the trilogy was dedicated to the Oneiros named Phantasos, who rules the area of inanimate objects and forces of nature within the design of dreams. Within his live drawing performance, that took place after dark and which was projected on the walls of the gallery in order to be followed, Viron Erol Vert not only responded to the unfolding sound collage at »Dreamatory«. Within the constant act of drawing and increasingly overlapping lines of varying ductus, there was also the attempt to transcend a level of rationality in order to approach a logic of dreaming in which the mind moves freely and leaps from one thought to the next.

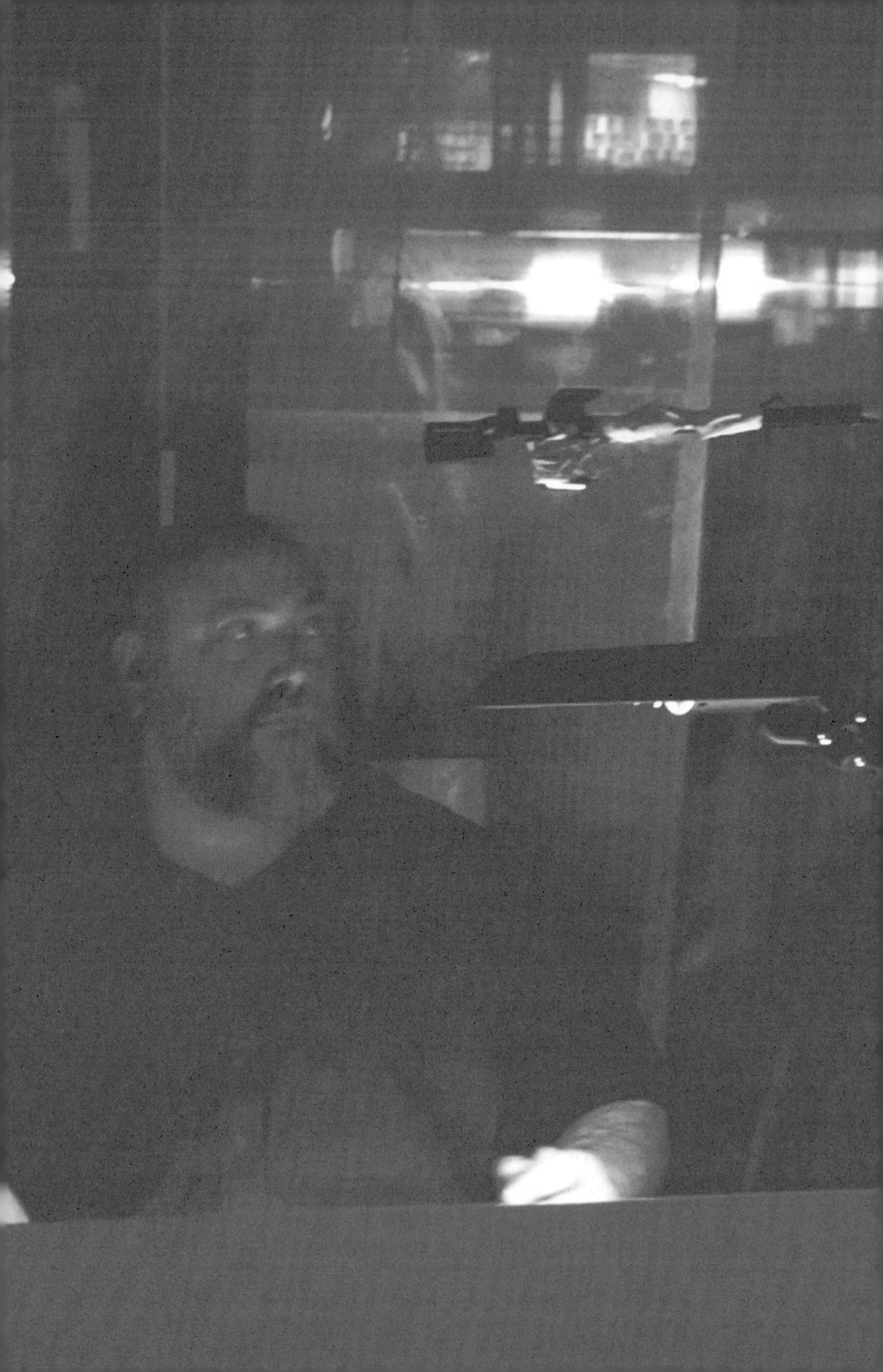

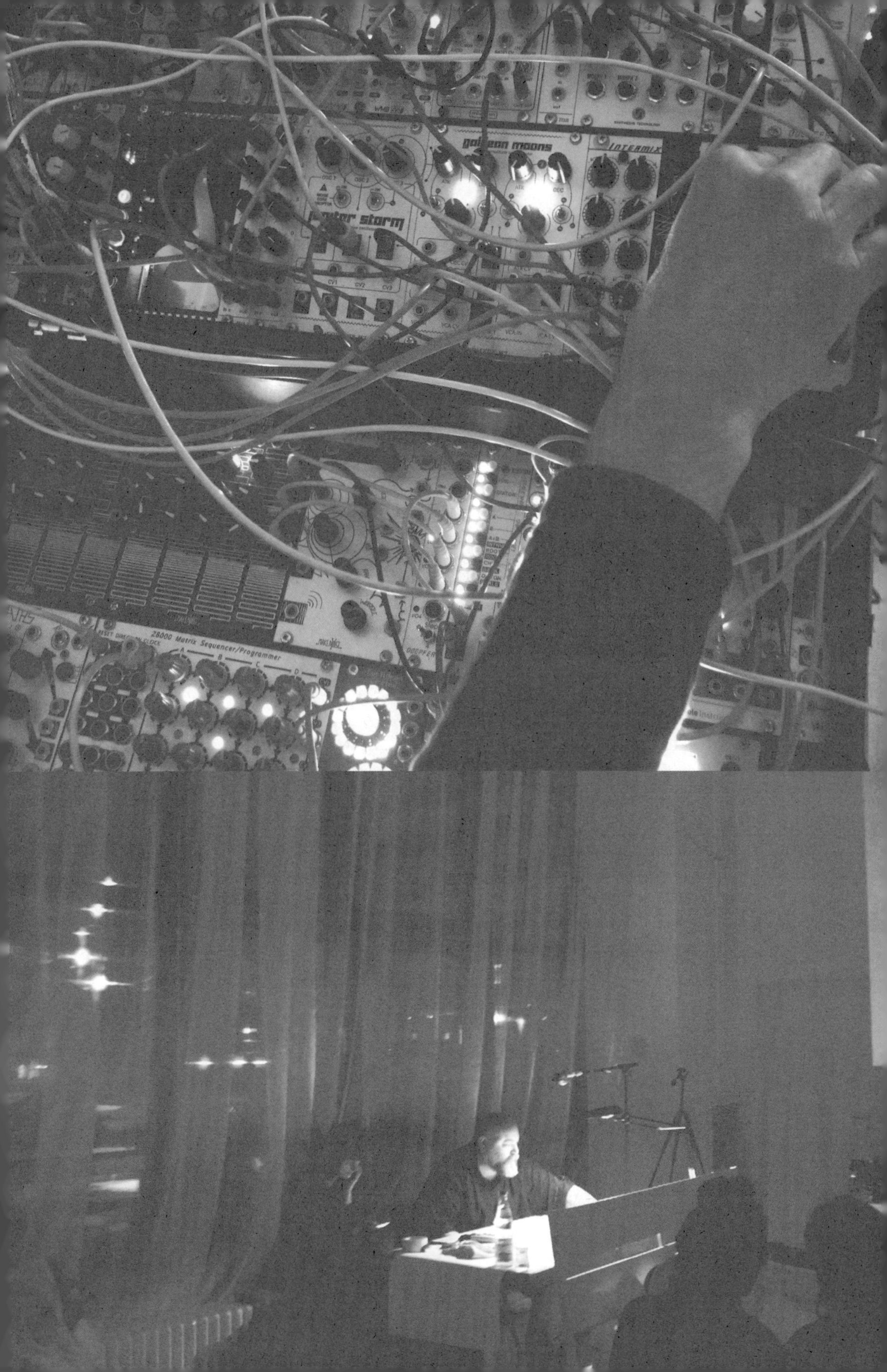
INTERMIX
DEC
CV1
CV2
CV3
28000 Matrix Sequencer/Programmer

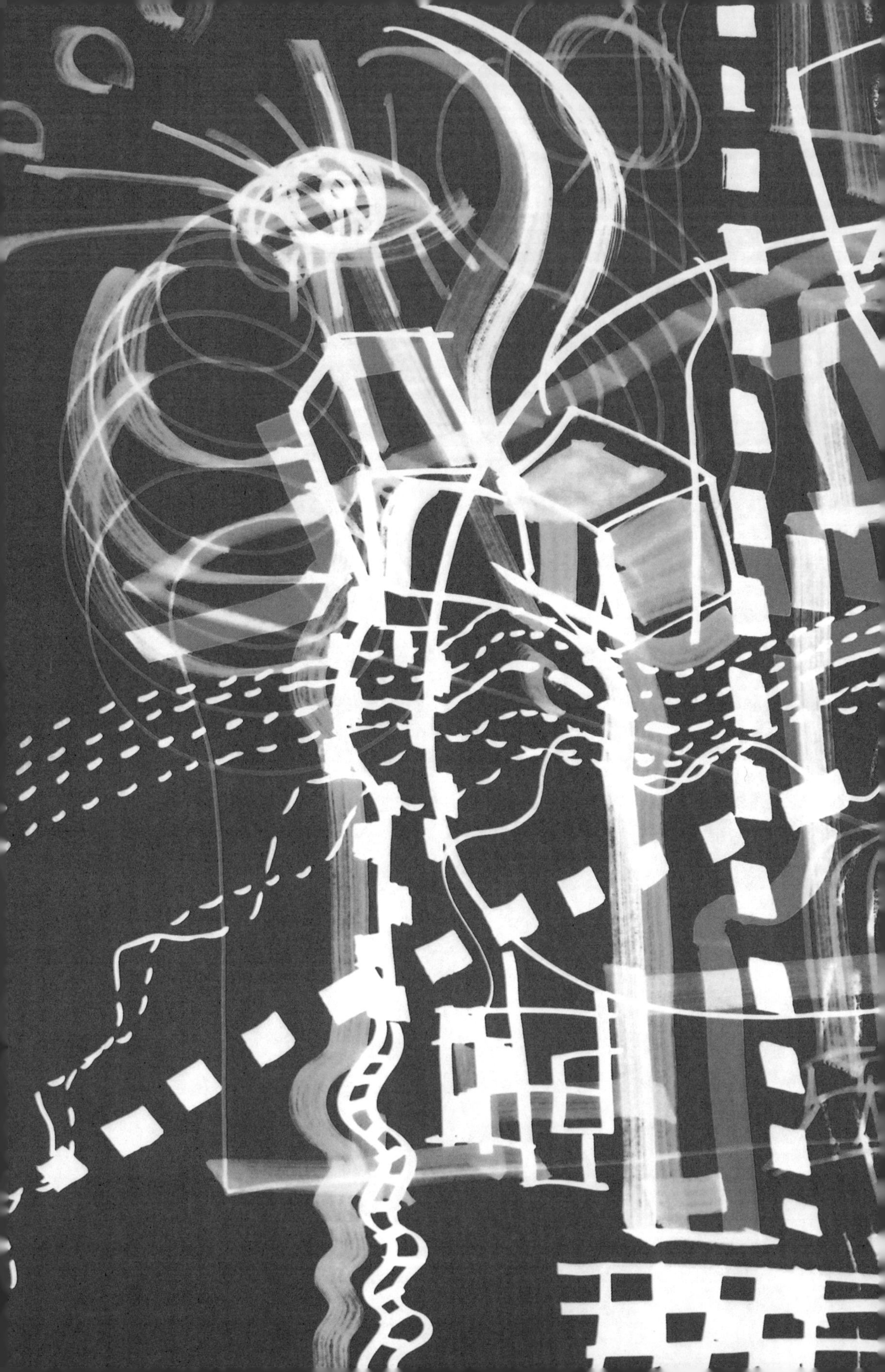

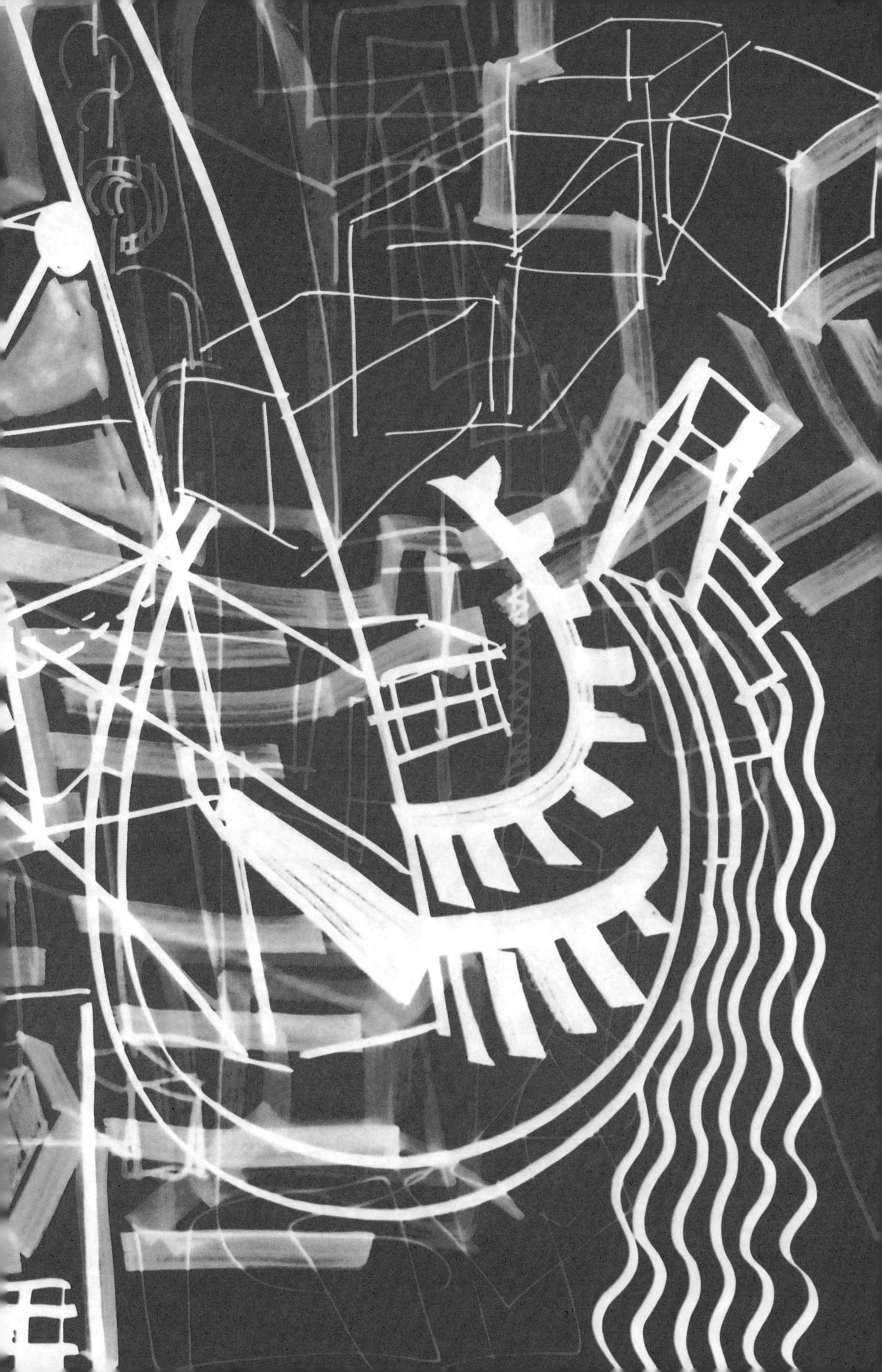

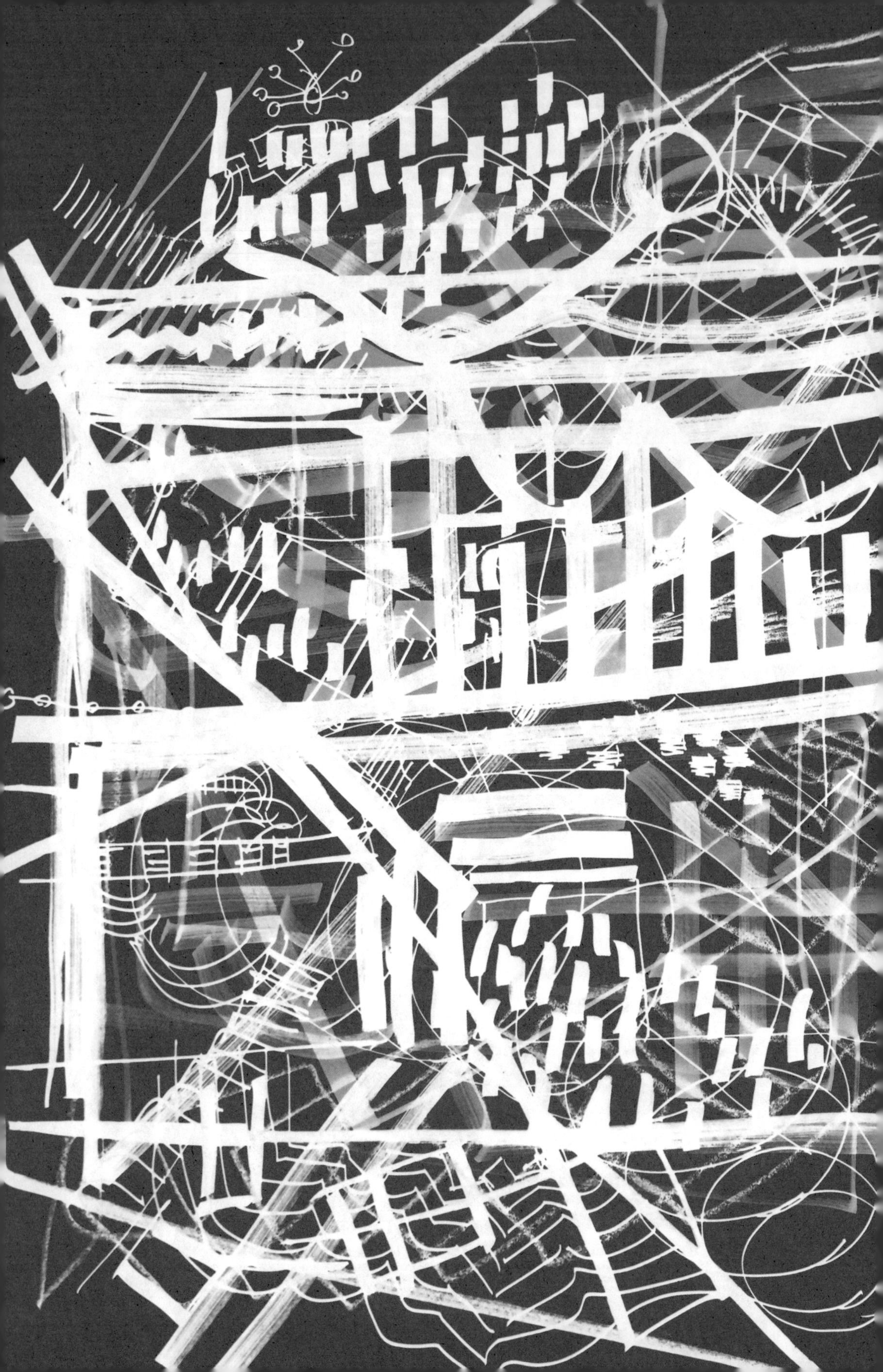

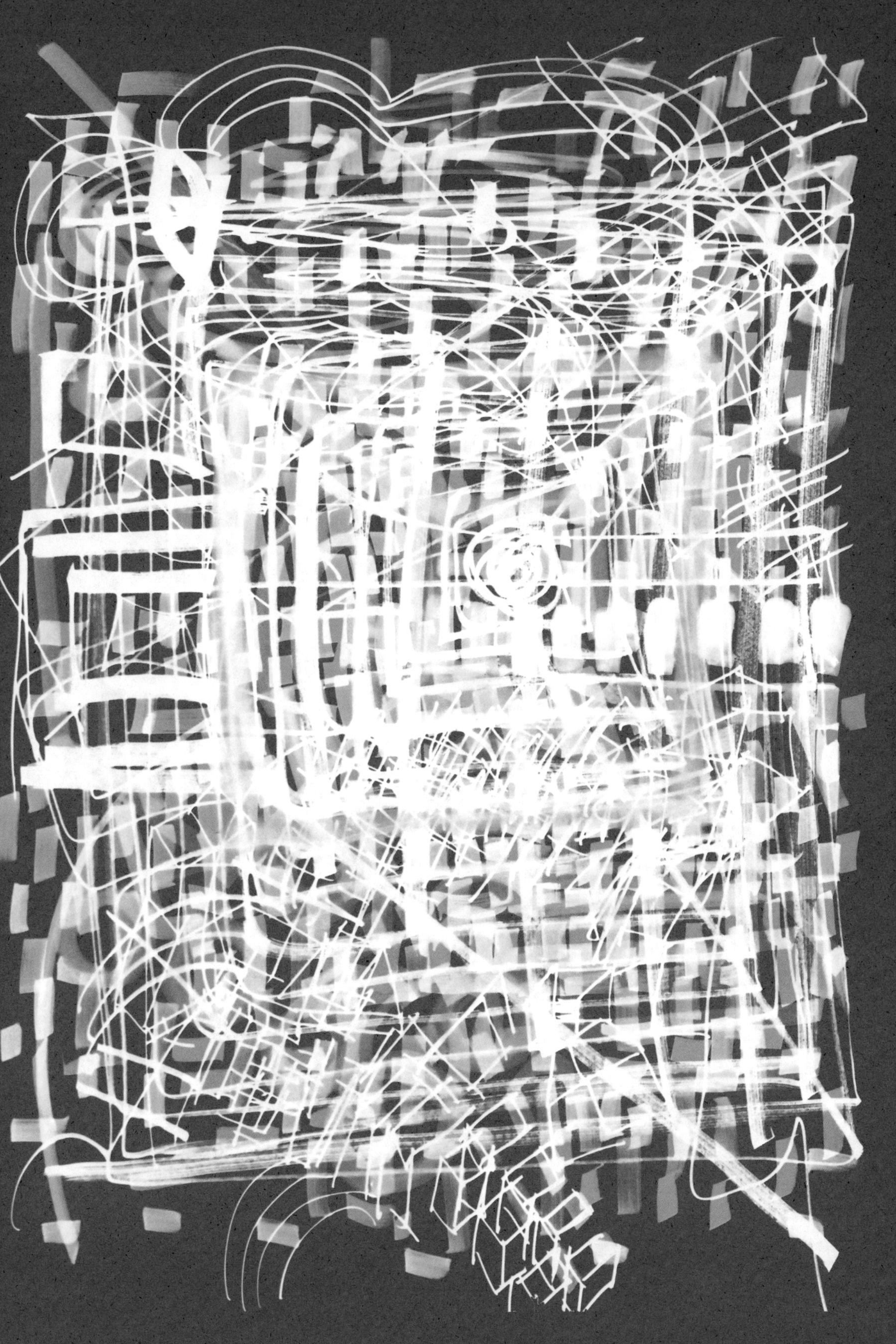

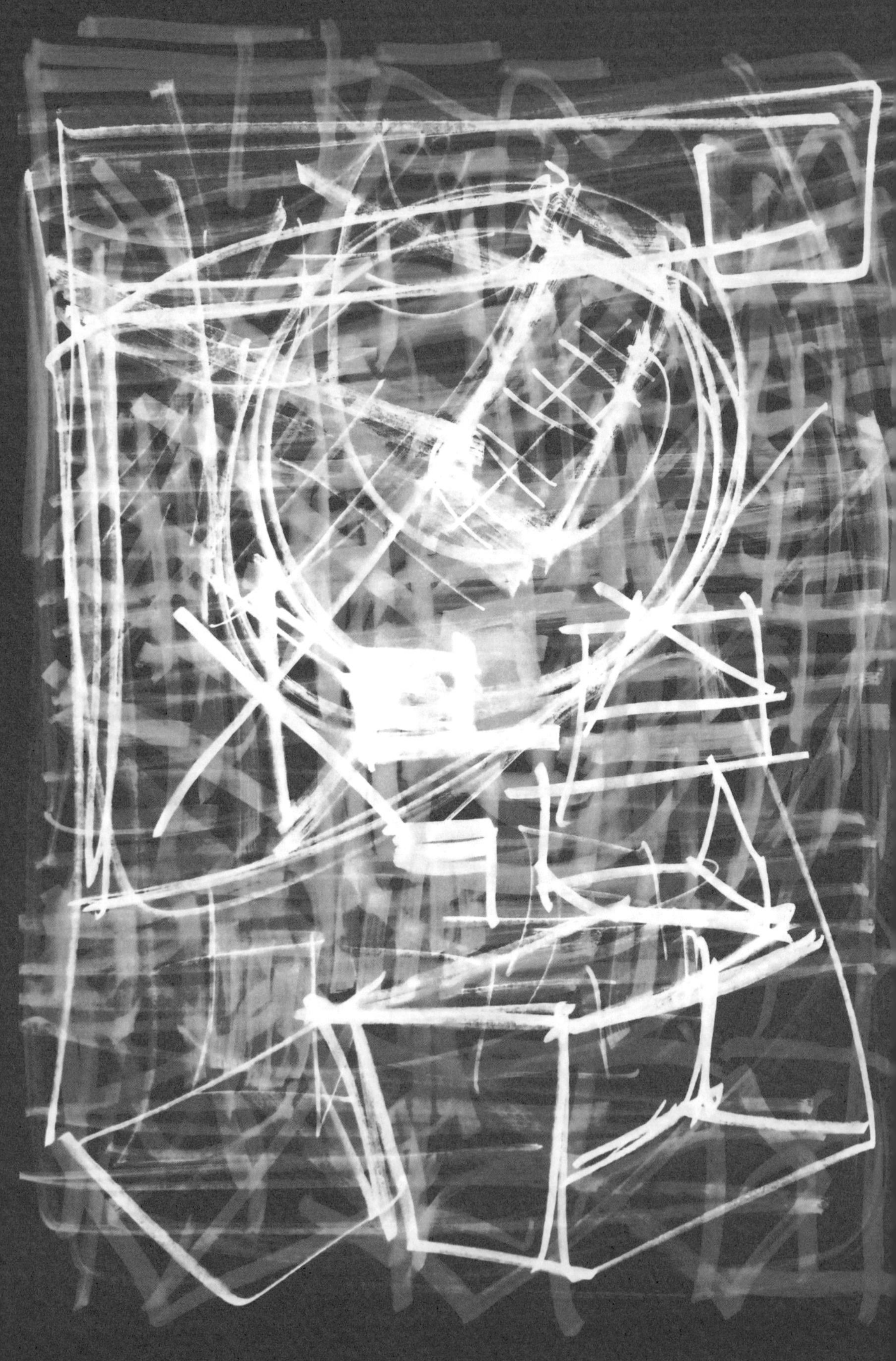

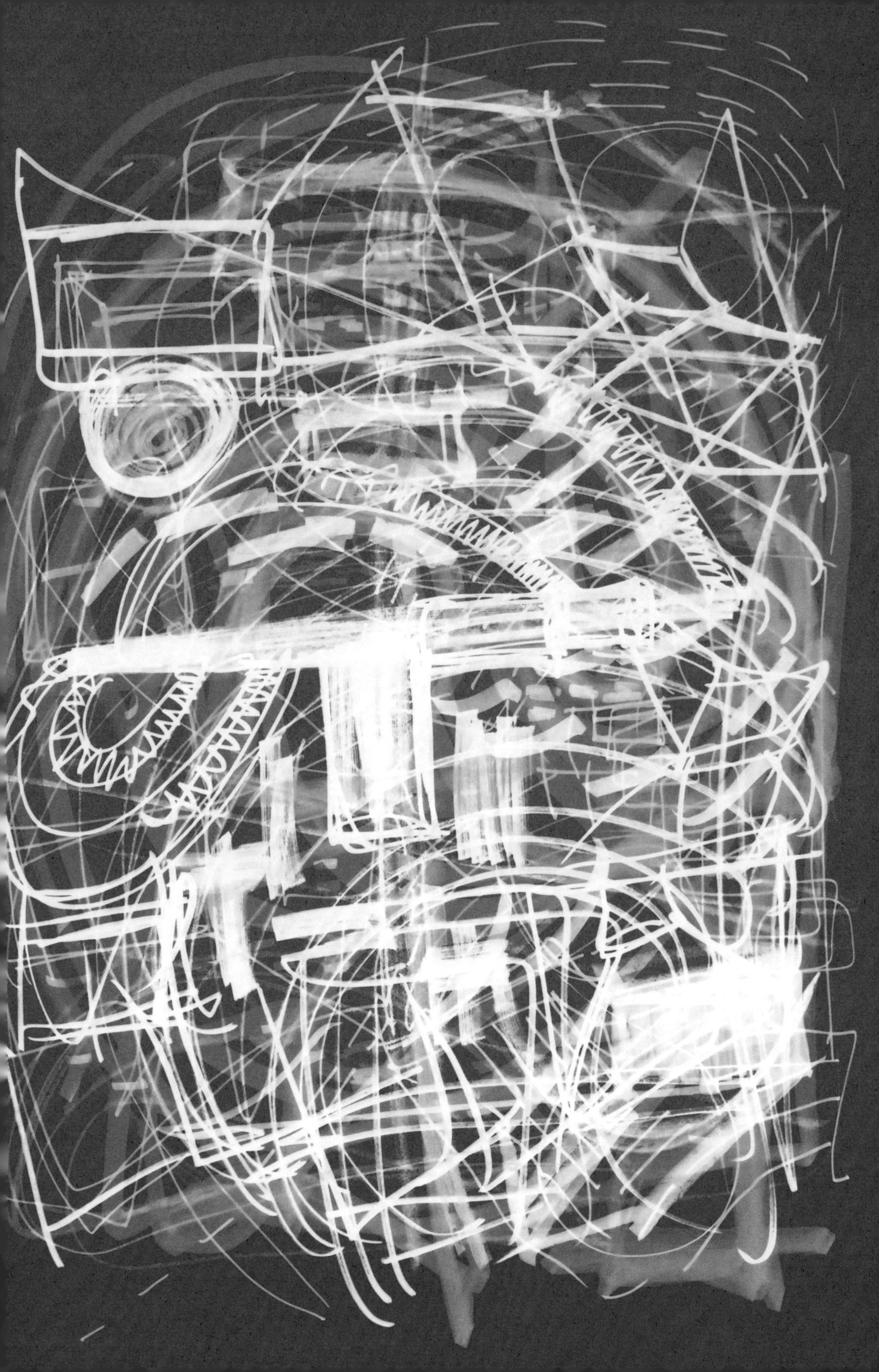

FLiegen & Tieger sein.
& Schöltröte sein.
& Krokodid sein.

DREAMATORY

DE

Während der gesamten Laufzeit von Verts Traumlabor in der Galerie Wedding bestand für dessen Besucher*innen die Möglichkeit, ihre Träume und die damit verbundenen Gedanken auf vorgefertigten Formularen zu manifestieren, festzuhalten und mitzuteilen. So entstand eine Sammlung von Träumen, die in Auszügen bereits auf Infobildschirmen in der U-Bahn veröffentlicht wurde. Sie bildet den Querschnitt eines kollektiven Traumbewusstseins, das im »Dreamatory« zutage treten konnte.

EN

Throughout the whole duration of Vert's »Dreamatory« at Galerie Wedding, the visitors were given the opportunity to manifest, capture and communicate their dreams and thoughts on forms. The result was a collection of dreams that has already partly been published on information screens in the subway. They form a cross section of a collective dream consciousness that was able to come to light at the »Dreamatory«.

wirkt aufwendig / Erlebnisraum

Vorort

nah Galerie / Schloß

Alleinerziehende Elternteil m. Kind

~~Ast~~rid Lindgrens Haus wohnen = Positives Gefühle dafür

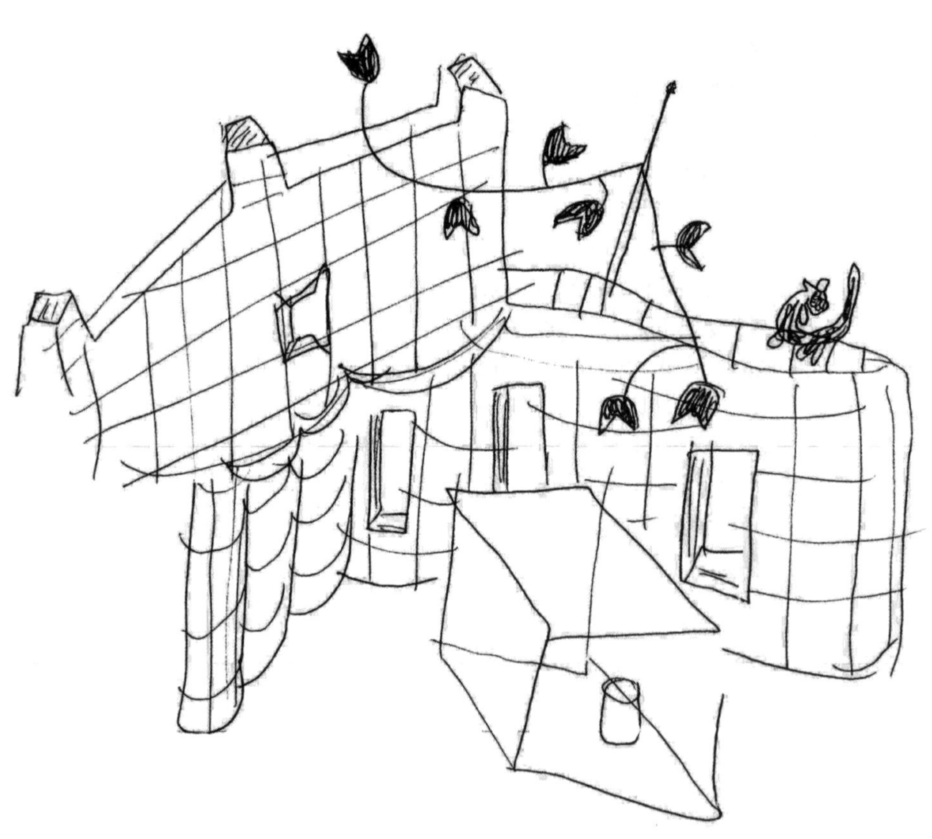

So blöd dass auch klingt, mein Traum seit 9 Jahren ist es eine Einladung von Karl Lagerfeld zur seiner Modenschau in Paris zu bekommen. Ich schreibe regelmäßig Briefe an ihn, ohne Erfolg.

Mein zweiter Traum ist der Frieden auf der Welt und die Lebenslust und die Akzeptanz der Menschen. Das Leben ist gut zu uns und wir sollen sie entdecken und schätzen.

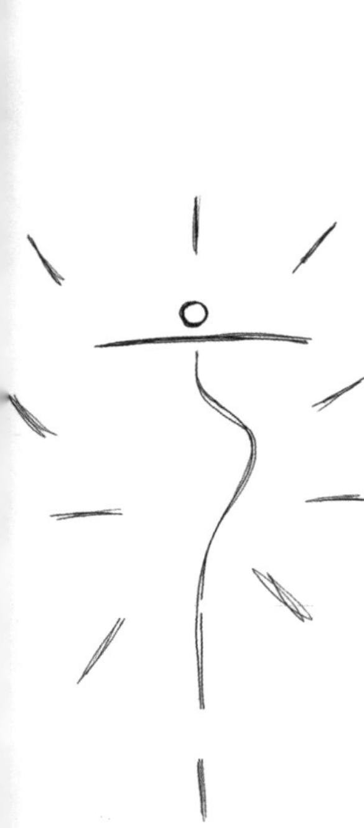

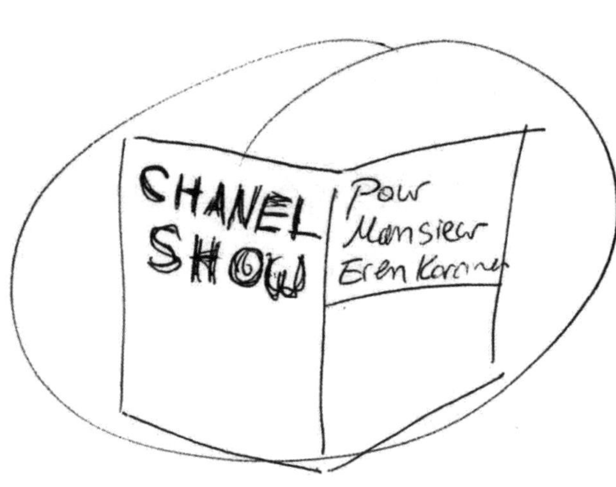

· 3 Personen im Freien
Ich, eine Frau, ein Arzt
Sie spricht über ihre Schmerzen in der Schulter. Der Arzt stürzt auf mich los. Mit vorgestreckten Armen und drückt heftig auf meine rechte Schulter.

Ich erwache am Morgen danach und spüre, dass meine Schulterunbeweglichkeit (seit $1\frac{1}{2}$ Jahren vorhanden) auch Schmerzen) fast verschwunden ist.

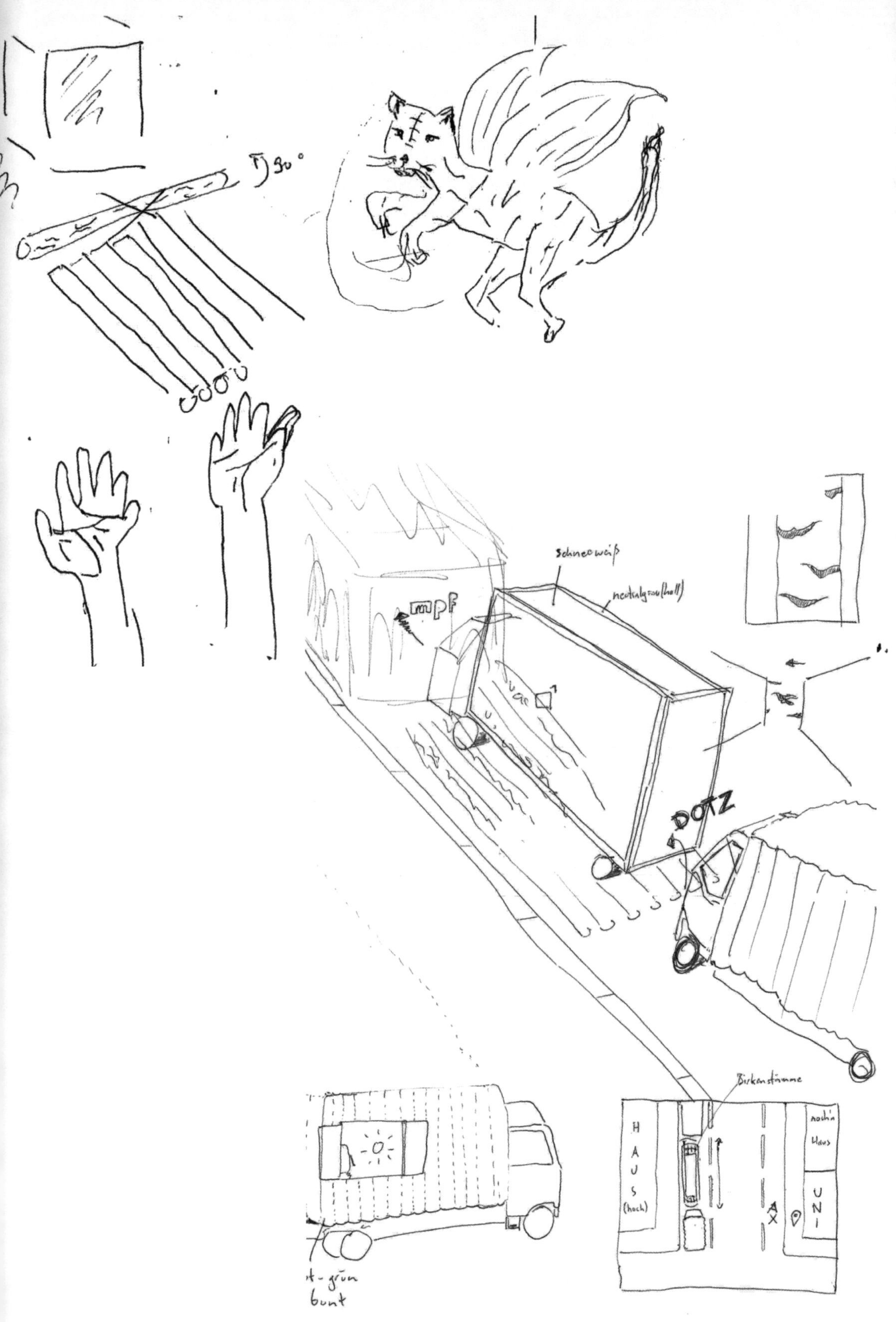
mpf
schneeweiß
DOTZ
Birkenstämme
HAUS (hoch)
noch'n Haus
UNI
bunt

I met my brother in a bath room and he was picking his ear with a Q-tip. He told me that things were not so okay and it was a wonder that he survived the operation/surgery

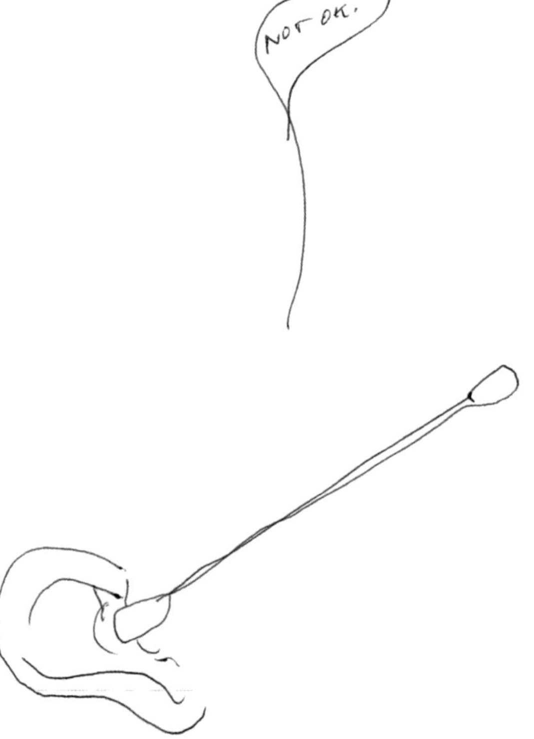

Wir waren Figuren in einem Kartenspiel. Ich war Spielerin und Figur gleichzeitig. Es gab jeden mehrmals. ~~[illegible]~~ z.b. war ein Ritter ein Freund. Es spiegelte sich die Karten bildeten Räume gleichzeitig konnte man jeder und jede betreten. Jemand sprang aus einer Karte auf mich zu ich sprang gleichzeitig in die Wirklichkeit und wachte auf

Ich bin meinem Freund auf eine Party fremdgegangen; er wohnt weit weg von mir und wir reden nicht oft bzw. <u>er</u> redet nicht viel. Aber dann ist e plötzlich zu mir gekommen und war sauer. Er hatte es erfahren (wir haben eine telepatische Verbindung im realen Leben). Dann hat e gesagt er will Karriere machen als Detektiv. Er ist im realen Leben DJ.

I was walking over a bridge. There was a guy in front of me. I was following. I wanted to call him, but I had no voice. Increasing my pace, I finally got close. ~~to him~~. I could only see his back. He wore a hoodie. I tapped his shoulder. He turns around. ~~I~~ He had my face. I wake up, scared ~~to~~ like hell.

~~Ez, [illegible], Ma~~

Mi film temaşa kerde û
Şîyo Xoja! Keye di, tiştepa
Kerenşî şerdi... Keber hêdî hêdî
abya şew kowne ama ni ser
Zê Dareta ayşaye (Dareta unkerese
mina kewtiya) Ez tersa, lerzena...
kiştêna awan şiyê nêbena nohauno
kiştêrce veşî têrsena, Mi destê
xo kerdi pêtê a û girêya...
Dareta, Dareta...

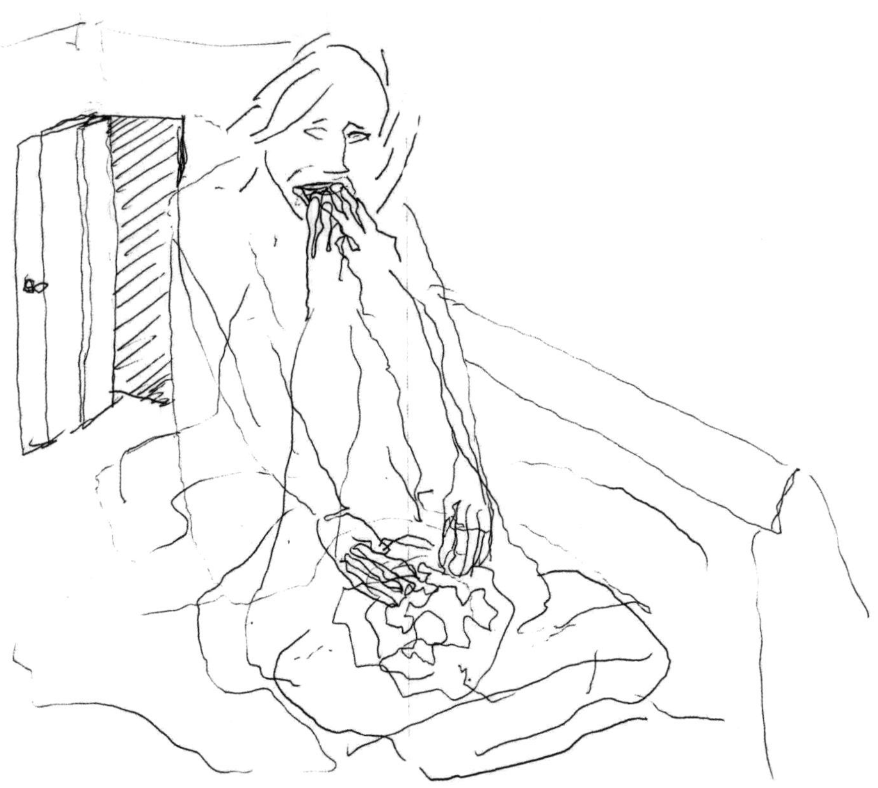

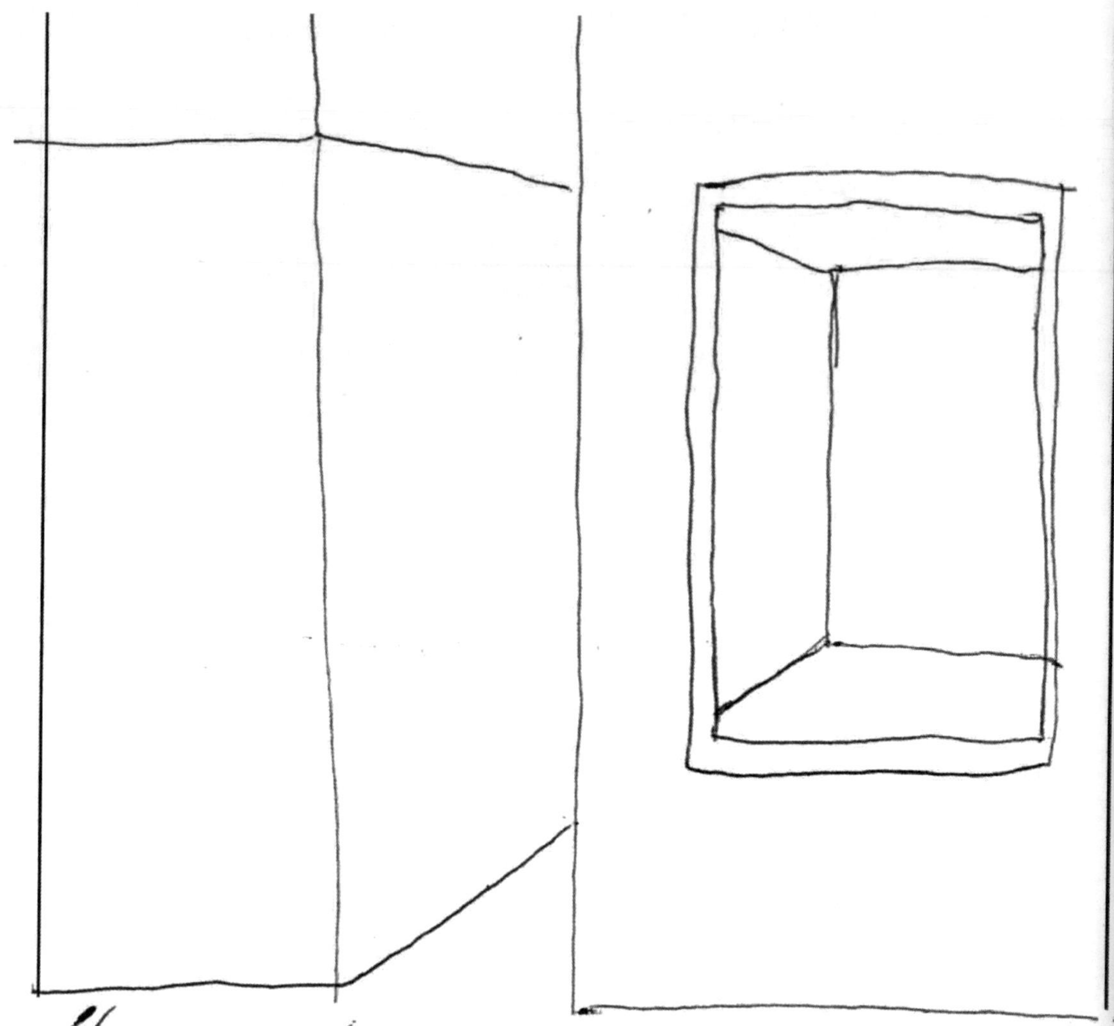

I'm in a hospital. Both, boyfriend and Sister, are very ill. I search for them. I allways miss them and fai to see them. Allways empty Rooms an doctors and nurses who are of scriving me the places were my sister are my friend might be.

Ich lief eine Straße entlang, es war menschenleer. Ich spürte, etwas stimmt nicht. Dann sah ich die Gestalten am Wegesrand, glibbrige, stachelige Aliens. Ich erinnerte mich, dass ich auch fliegen kann, also nahm ich Anlauf und flog weg. Ich begegnete anderen fliegenden Menschen. Dann wurde ich müde, machte Pause. Ich fand einen kleinen Ministaubsauger, auf dem ich weiterflog. So war es einfacher.

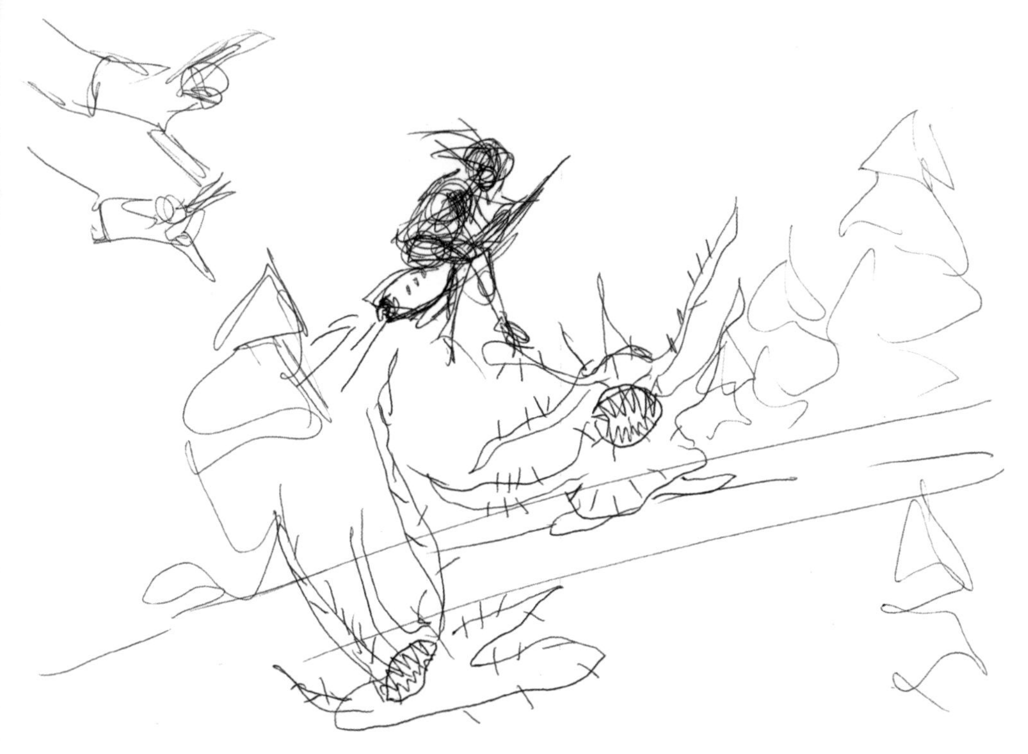

Einmal habe ich davon geträumt, dass ich Verkäuferin war in einem Sportschuhladen. Irgendwann sind Guns 'n' Roses reinspaziert und ich habe einen ~~[illegible]~~ von der Band (ich glaube den Bassist) überzeugt ultramarinblaue Fußballschuhe zu kaufen.

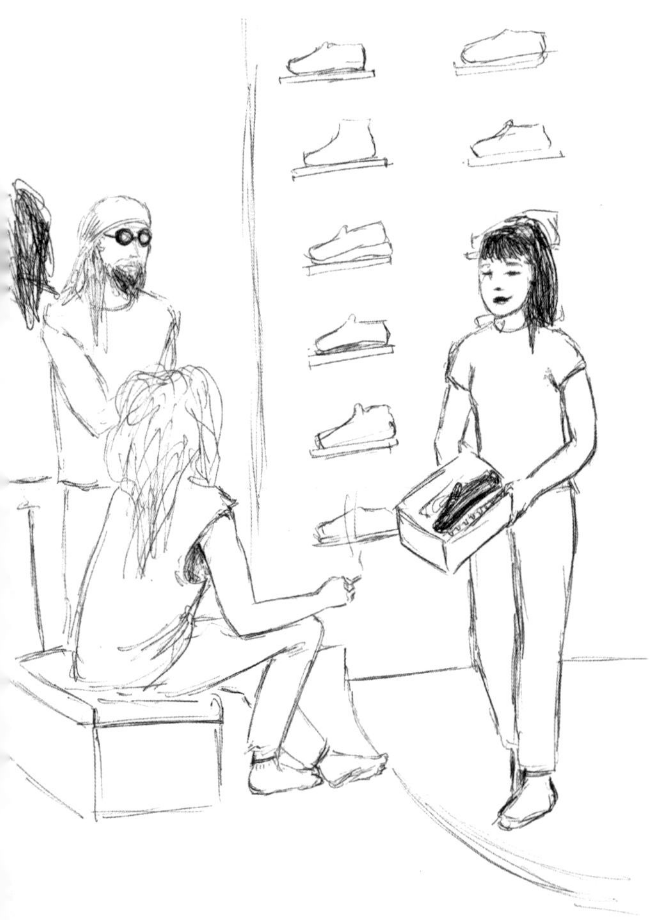

Me and Karl are crossing a bridge. It's slippery, long and unstable. Beneath us are a dark and deep lake. Somehow I can feel the depth of it by looking at it, something like vertigo. We hold on to eachother tightly and walk determinently towards the other side. We don't talk to eachother but we know instinctively that our only option is forward. There is both a sense of fear and a sense of hope, as if something was chasing us to the other side, the safer side. It starts to rain and the bridge gets even more slippery. Every step is a risk and I feel encreasingly frightened. All of a sudden I realize we reached the other side. Nothing feels different. I'm still scared and the old ground beneath me doesn't comfort. I wake up.

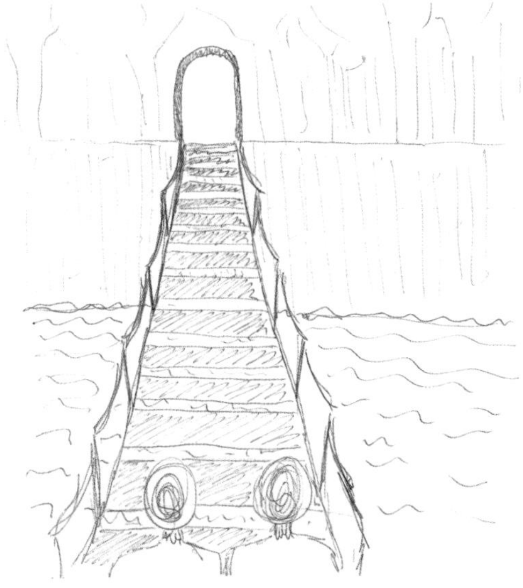

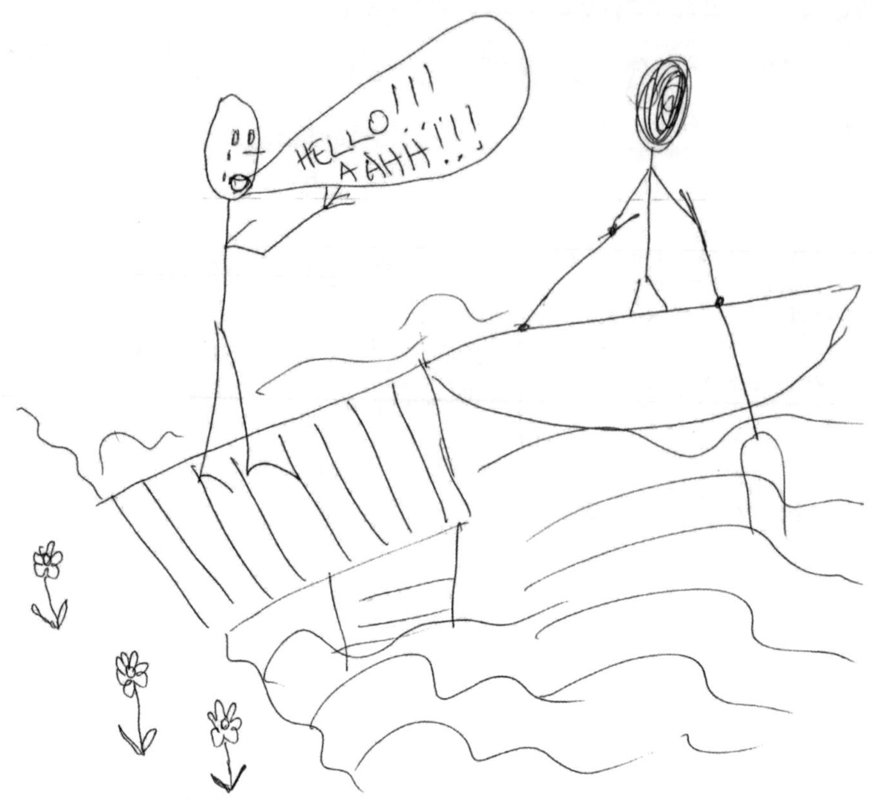

I saw my dead father on his lovely boat. I talked to him but he couldn't see me, I couldn't hear me. He was alive infront of me (IRL he had been dead for 5 years) but he didn't notice me, I was like air. I have dreamt that thing for many years, now it's 16 years since he died. I always woke up with a horrible feeling and can't breath normally.

A man calm walking in a very long aisle. Everything is dark, but you can see a lot of closed doors. Suddenly the man runs, always faster... someone appears behind him

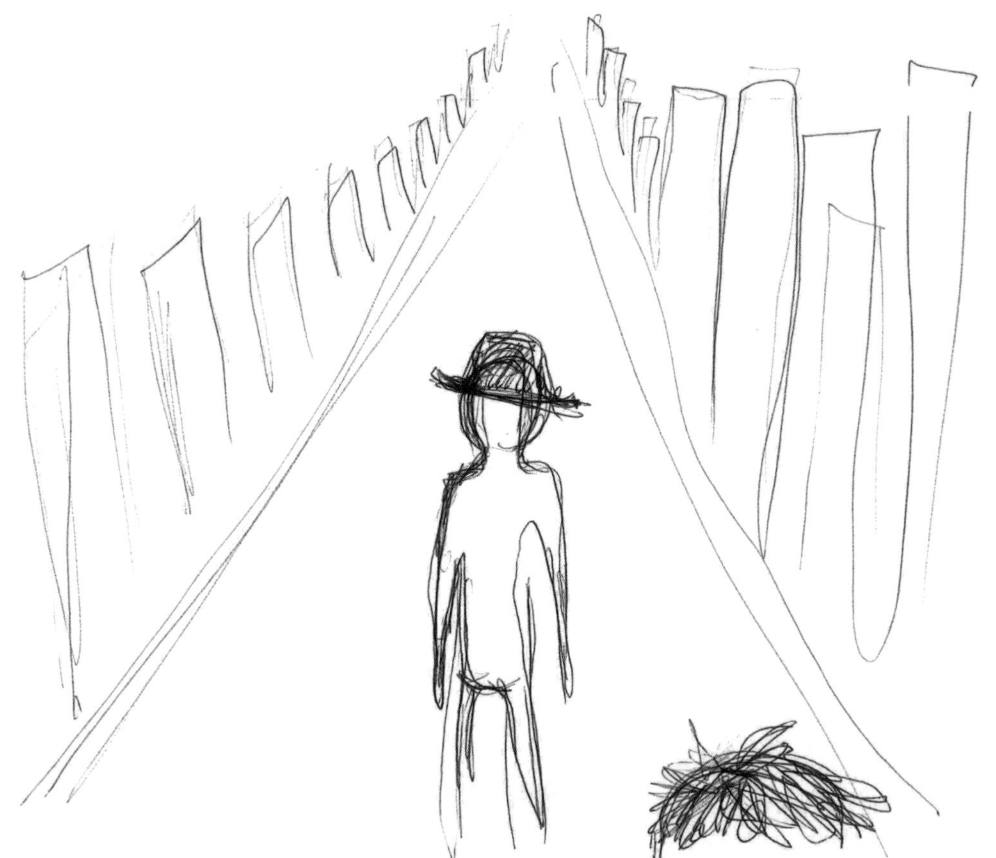

I'm in a space shuttle, in a big white bedroom without any piece of ~~for~~ furniture. I'm the captain of the shuttle and I'm ill.

A little old man enters the door and asks me how I'm doing and updates me on the latest universe's news. I take the pills he brings me and explode in a thousand stars, spreading throughout the whole universe.

Ein ständig wiederkehrender Traum: Ich bin im Urlaub, mit meiner Freundin oder mit meinen Elter und es ist der letzte Tag, die Rückreise steht an, abe ich bzw. wir sind schon so spät dran, dass ich es gar nicht mehr zum Flugzeug oder Zug schaffen kann. Es ist schon eine Art Angsttraum, aber eine milde Sorte davon denke ich...

Last night, I dreamt that I took a full LSD slide.
I have never taken LSD before
I rememeber ~~sat~~ my fear
after ~~having~~ of the consequence
I don't remember anything else
from the dream.

Früher würde allgemein behauptet, man träume nür schwarz-weiß. Ich hatte einmal irgend einen Traum, währenddessen ich eindeütig eine bünte Szene erlebte. Im Traum würde mir bewüsst, dass die obige These als nicht stimmt.

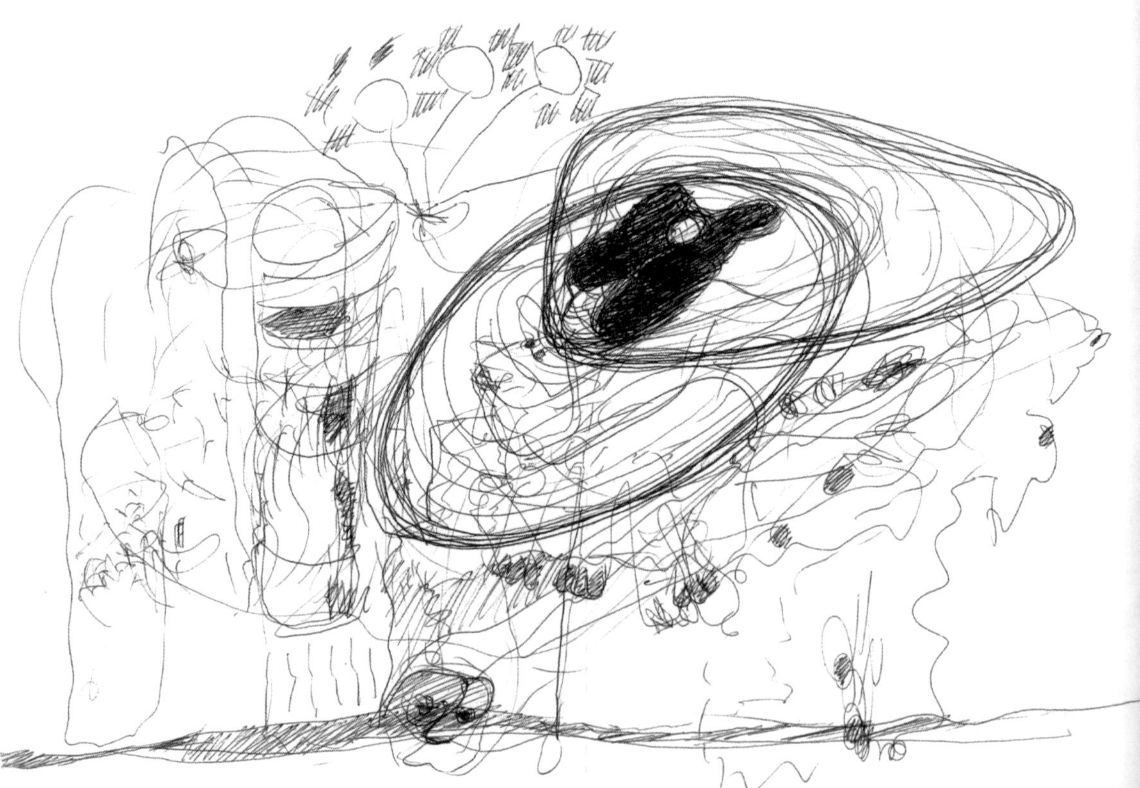

A night sky, dark, but millions of stars. They don't differ in shape or colour, white dots in the sky, the universe above me.

Then I realise that I'm standing in front of a cherry tree – the white stars turned into white blossoms of the tree.

I am astonished and delighted about the change.

I continue to look up and try to count the blossoms, but they're too many. Therefore I just wonder.

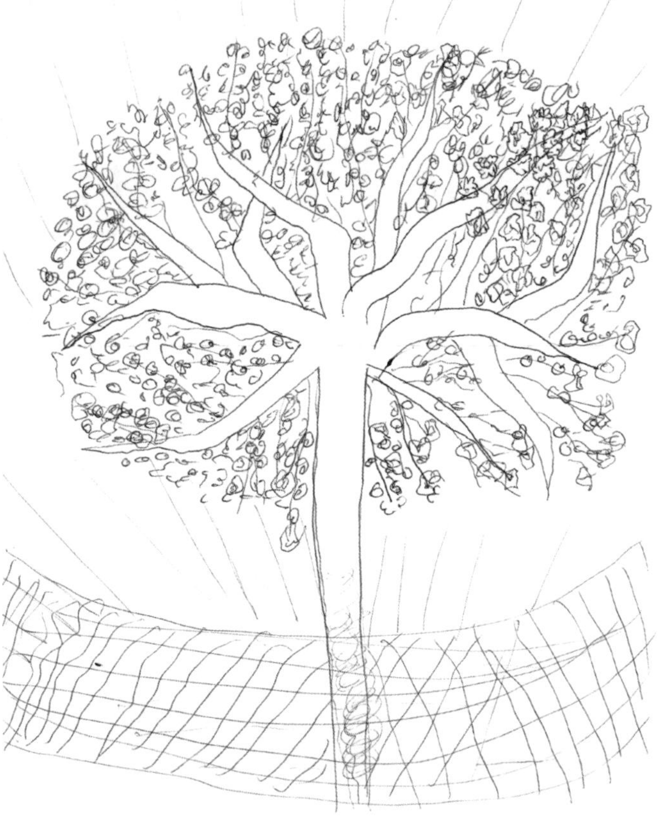

I often have this dream, that a little grey mouse eats my toes. When I wake up screaming, she flies away...

everything was laser green.

Dream of
what can happen
in reality as if you
are dreaming.

I mean → how to live
in "day world" but
be in the state as if
you constantly see
dreams and know it.

A man draped in black offered me three glass jars filled with a bubbling liquid: one red, one yellow and one cyan. I chose the yellow liquid and drank greedily from the jar. I was transformed into a waning moon with no understanding of time. I brought the tides into my arms and sent them crashing back to shore. I dreamt I was some god of the sea... but who was this god in black who granted me my godhood?

dream of a dream of a realm of a cream of a land for dream of a of one but common but for all a dream of all for all

Ich beneide alle, die die Fähigkeit besitzen,
sich an ihre Träume zu erinnern.
Träume sind für mich mit eine der wichtigsten
Faktoren, die die Schlafqualität beeinflussen.
Gute Träume geben einen das Gefühl, erholt
zu erwachen. Alpträume dagegen machen die Erholung
des Schlafes zunichte.
Seit Jahren erinnere ich mich schon nicht mehr an
meine Träume, allerdings gibt es den einen Traum
aus meiner Kindheit, den ich abrufen kann, als
hätte ich ihn soeben "erlebt.
Es war ein Albtraum. Ich sitze auf meinem
Kinderbett und mein Vater kommt in mein Zimmer.
Er gestikuliert, spricht, ohne dass ich verstehen kann,
was er sagt.
Ein Quadrat öffnet sich in der Mitte des Zimmerbodens
und er fällt. Flammen züngeln aus dem Loch.
Ich trauere im Traum, weil ich weiß, dass mein Vater
zu schlecht war und das seine Strafe ist.
Katholische Erziehung verrückt das Weltbild.

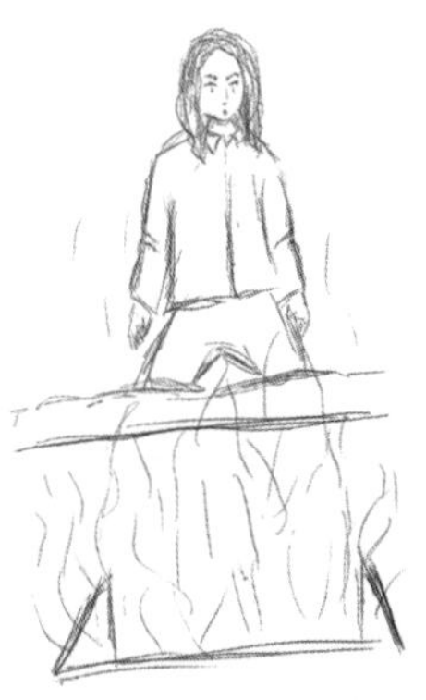

I hardly remember the dreams. But two nights ago I did. I woke up after talking with the new lefty predident party. There is at the moment a lot of conflict and different factions. I dreamt I was talking with him and saying that they should relax, we depend on their moves.

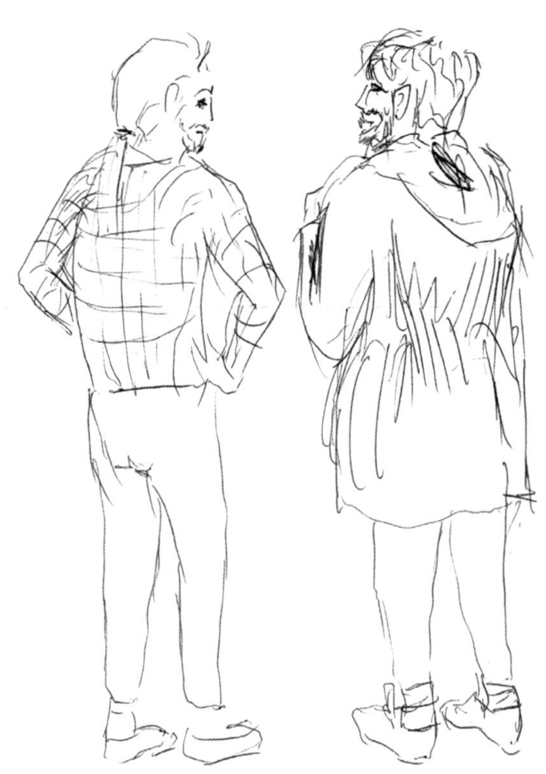

Ich sitze auf einer Schaukel.
es gibt keine Welt.
Ich ~~schaukel~~ schwinge in die
schwerelosigkeit. es ist ein
gutes gefühl im bauch. ~~wenn~~
ein gefühl von ewigkeit.
wenn da nicht die angst
vor dem aufpral wäre,
die sich im kopf festsetzt
und ~~noch~~ immer stärker wird,
je länger der traum anhält.

Weltraum,
Loop.
Elemente
Linie
bunt.
Ich bin allein,
sie sind alleine,
Laufend,
schwebend,
Raum,
Zeit,
Endlos

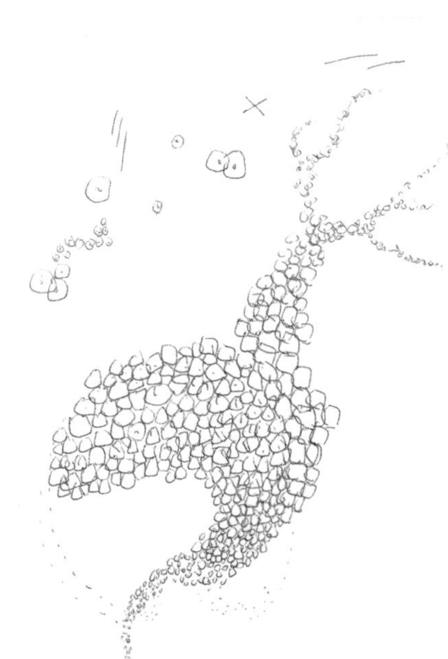

no paranoia,
but fluid, lucent,
cozy waves...

Fliegen & Tieger sein.
& Schöltröte sein.
& Krokodid sein.

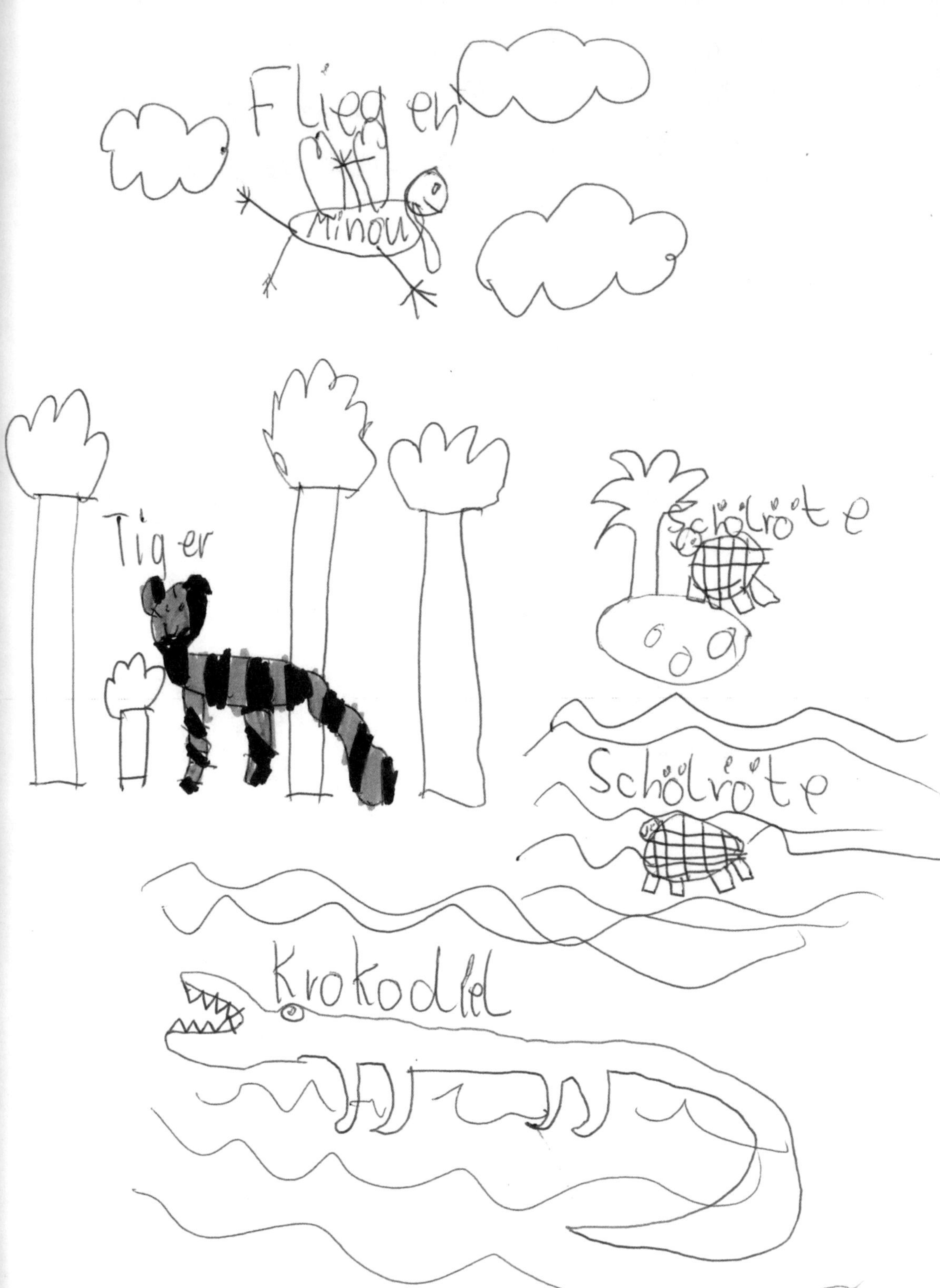
Fliegen
Minou
Tiger
Schölröte
Schölröte
Krokodlel

Ich war auf einer Insel
im Wald es hat geschneit.
Plötzlich war da eine Grube.
Also sprang ich rein und
ich war am Strand. Das
Wasser war Türkis blau grün
Ich fing an zu tauchen
Unter wasser war es wunder
schön da kam ein Fisch zu
mir und lächelte mich an
Ich konnte unter wasser
atmen. Also tauchte ich tiefer
und fand ein Korallenrif.
Dan war der Traum vorbei.

über mehrere Wendeltreppen habe
ich mit mehreren Freunden
und Bekannten gesprochen.

Ich gehe eine Straße entlang (vorwärts, alleine). Am Wegesrand liegen beidseitig unbekannte Leichen, deren Todesart nicht zu erkennen ist. Ich bin ratlos und schaue nach anderen noch Lebenden, aber es sind keine zu finden.

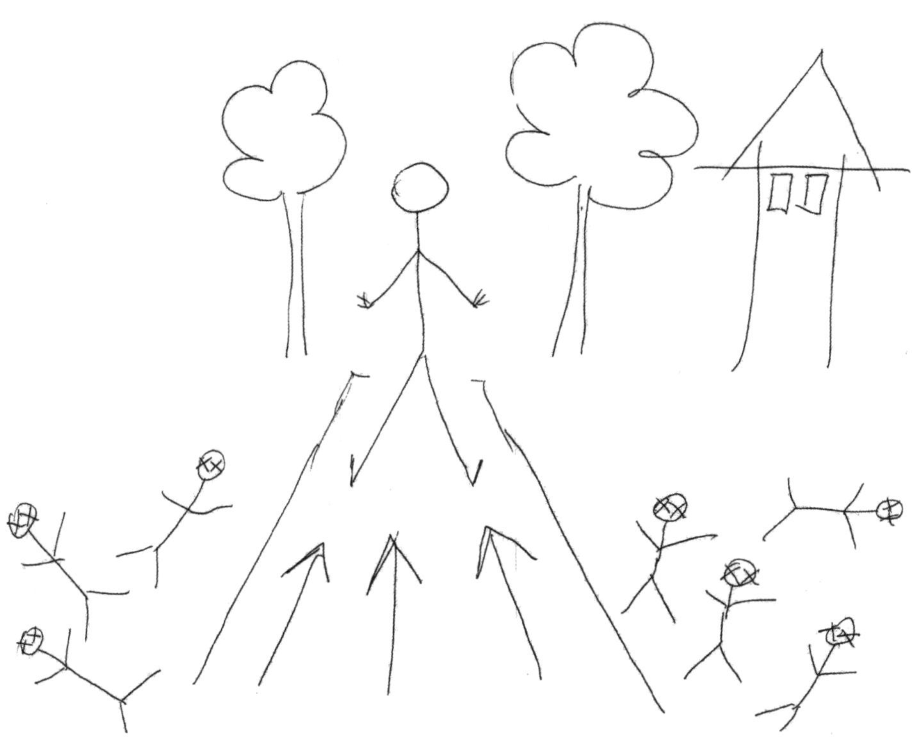

A humming bird flew into my ear and flew out my other ear

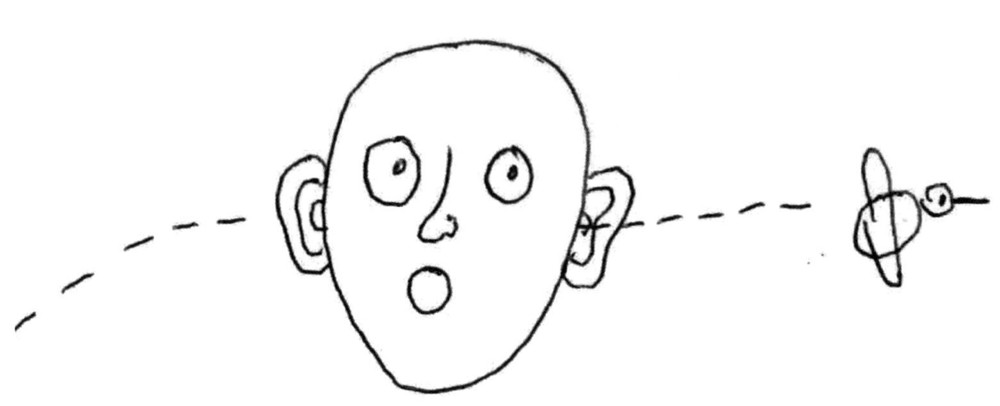

I had dreamed of a young man who had murdered someone, who + why is unclear to me now but there was a forest as well as a family meal.

I pull a ceramic pot from the grand. it is beautiful. The out-side is colorfull and the inside is black, with sure textres of color, like crushed candy. I touch there colors and the cut into the palms of my hands. I take them out of my hands and bleed. I am not in pain or scared. I am amazed that I am liquid inside.

One time I had a dream that I was an FBI agent chasing a serial killer. He kept escaping me and murdering people, and it made me very angry. When I finally caught him I pointed my gun at him aggressively. Suddenly I heard, "Babe," and I awoke to find that I had made my hand in the shape of a gun, and was pointing it ~~at~~ against my husband's head.

1. I was on a futon, relaxing, and an old friend named James walked up and tried to fold me up into the mattress. He was laughing a kind of fake evil laugh.

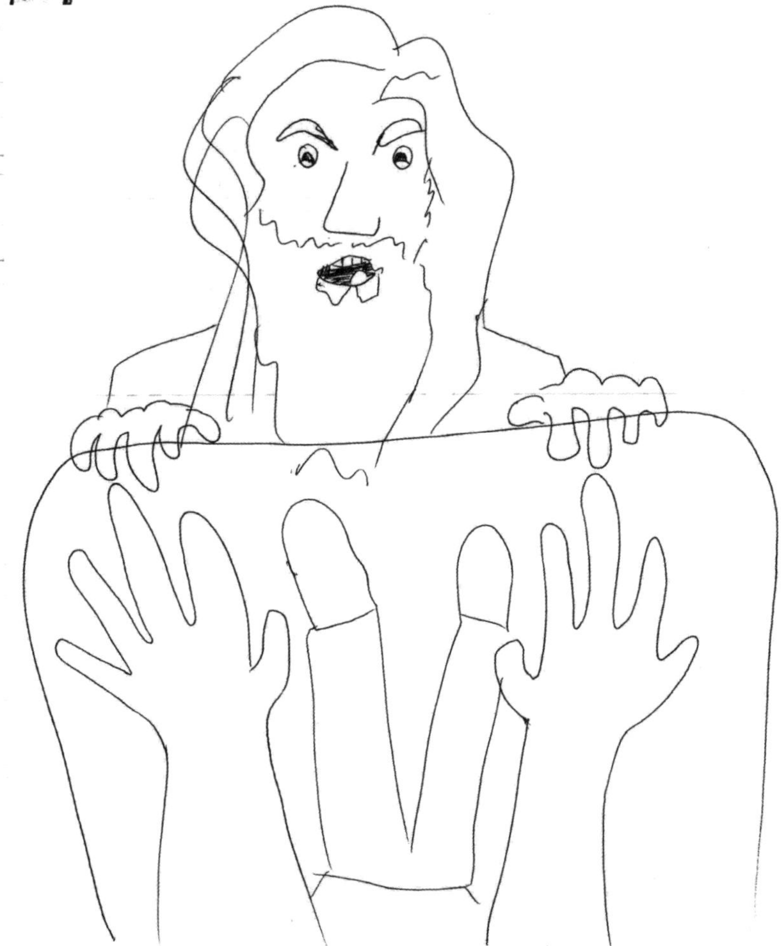

Ich sitze am Haven von Haitabu im vergangenden Zeitalter, auf einen Querliegenden Baumstamm. Ein Fremdländisches Handelsschiff mit roten Segel ankert vor mir.
Ein dunkles süßes Bier ist in meinen Trinkhorn. Ein korpulenter Händler Spricht mich an, ob ich nicht Wein probieren will, aus dem Fernen Süden. Ich leere mein Trinkhorn in einen zug und folge den korpulenten, Freundlichen Händler der in Elber Seide gekleidet ist, auf sein Schiff...

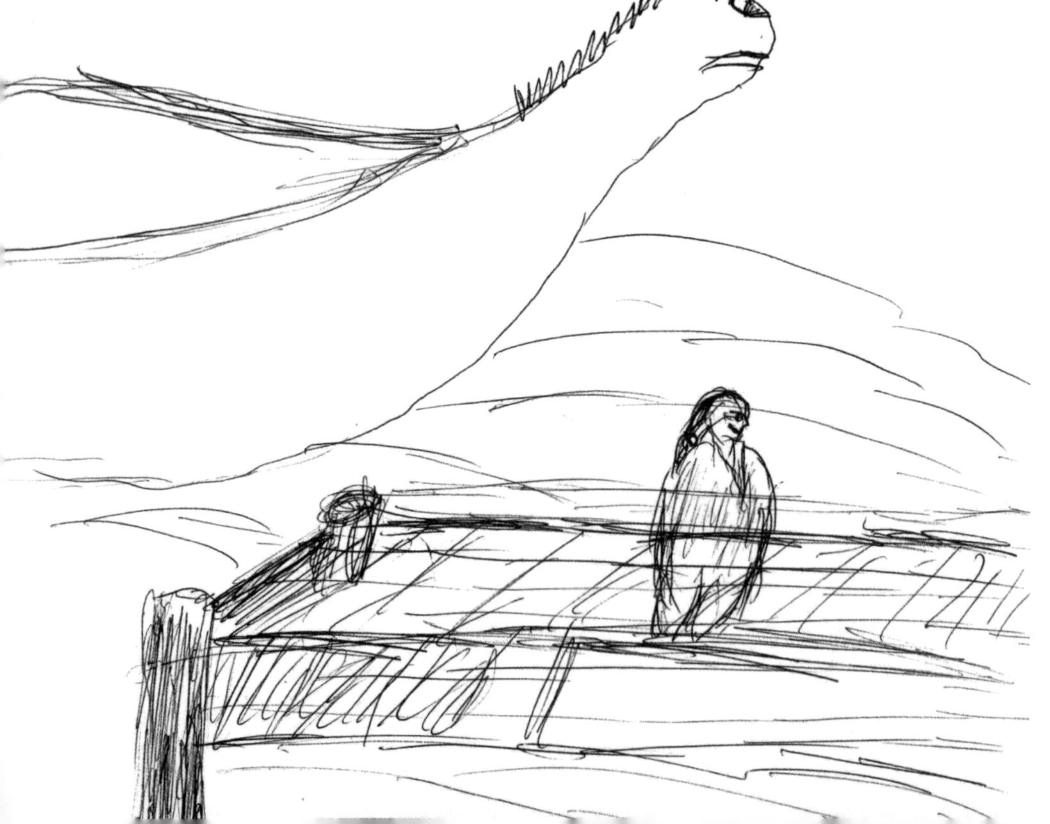

als ich 5-6-7 jahre alt war,
da lag ich in meinem bett
und erfühlte einen bewegten
Vogel, innerlich, ich sah ihn,
dachte an ihn und wurde
zu ihm, der Vogel war auf
lebendem Feuer gemacht,
dies war seine essenz ...
Meine Umgebung verschwand
und ich war dieser fliegende
FeuerVogel

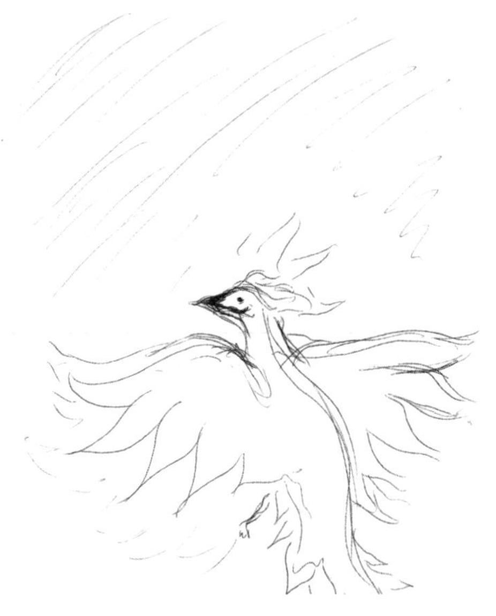

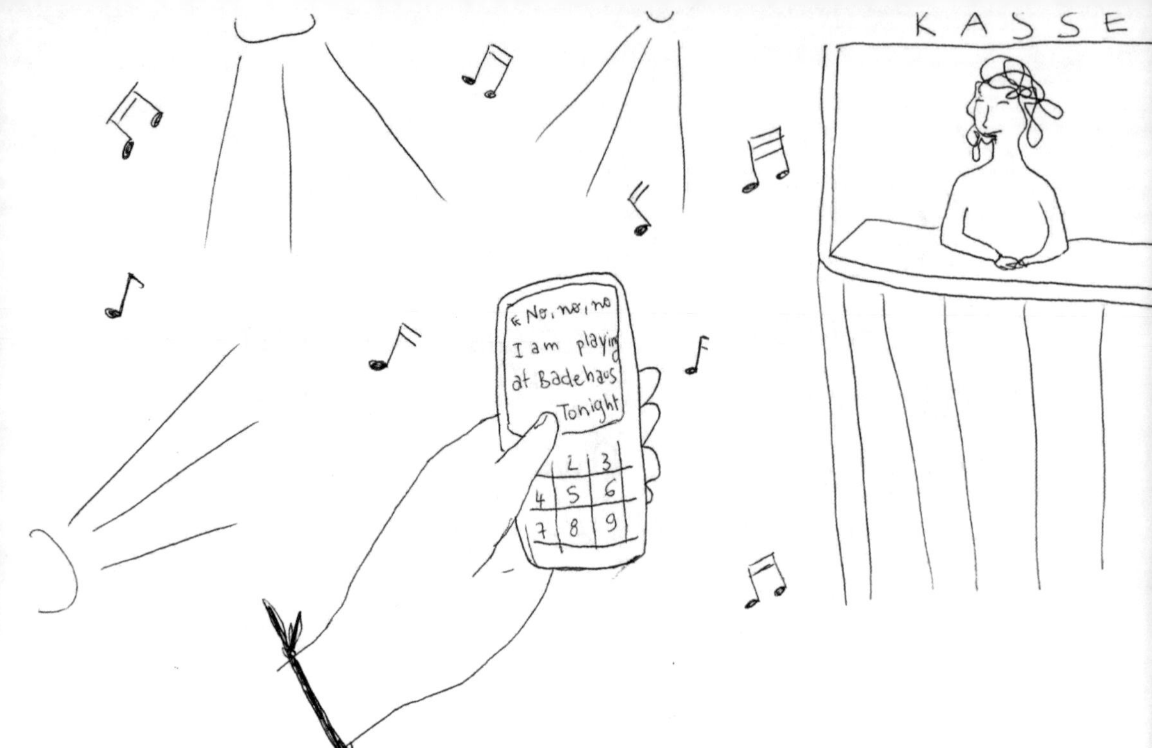

When I fall asleep, I was still waiting for an sms of a beautifful guy I met some days ago.

* * * * * *

I was in a party, with a good friend. Lot of music, lots of nice people, red lights, lots of different room. I couldn't see what was happening in the main party room, but I understood there was a live hip hop band playing.
I received an sms. It was him! Saying "No, no, no, I am playing at Badehaus tonight".
I get that he was the one playing in this party. I get scared and I left.

Reading Bliss Perry (b.1860) on Walt Whitman now to come down; "the Jacksonian period of our national existence" he writes. "Here are the roughs and beards and space and ruggedness and nonchalance the soul loves," Whitman writes + I think he is referring to Berlin-Wedding. The American poets are to enclose old + new for America is the race of races. Of them, a Bard is to commensurate with a people. To him the other continents arrive as contributions.

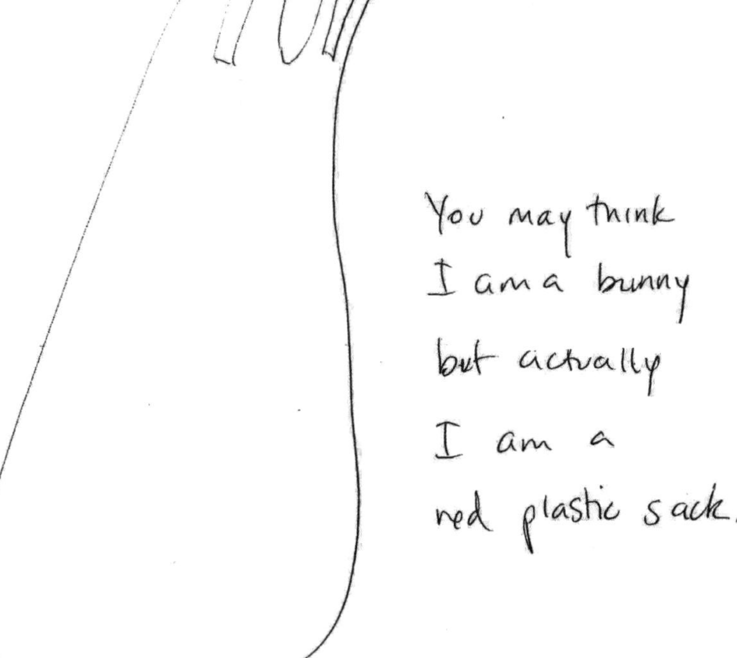

• Ich komme aus einer Salontür auf
einen riesigen Ami-Parkplatz
• Ich verfolge eine "Besessene". Sie ist
mager & klein. Ich verfolge sie, sie
springt von einem Auto-dach zum
anderen, schubst eine hoch schwangere
Frau zur Seite,
springt in ihren Kofferraum,
ich haue die Tür auf ihre
Beine, sehe ich bin ein alter
Mann, wie "Der Onkel" und Jäger.
Silberkugeln. Pflock, Weihwasser, etc.
~~Wir Spi~~
Es folgt noch ein Traum, ein
paar Wochen später.

Tag traum : Aufwachen, Blut im Stuhl
Kaffee am morgn – kaffee am Vormittag
ag. Entwicklungsgespräch zu/über
meine erste Tochter ! Panikattacke !
zusammen gerissen ! Farben ein
kaufen = jetzt im Bett liegen !
Erfolg !
Der
Künstler
hat
Zeit !

Pipi Neu
Y Lu Frida
Bimer
usw

Endlich Nichraucher !

Bimer
und die
Sieben
gesichter

Endlich
Nich
Raucher

Der Alptraum aus meiner Kindheit:

Dunkelheit – viele Baumstämme

Baumstämme, die auf einen zurasten. Immer wieder.

Als Kind bin ich oft deshalb hochgeschreckt.

Irgendwann hörte dies auf.

Inzwischen träume ich kaum noch schlecht.

darstellbar!?

(In meinen Träumen passiert oft sehr viel, wenn ich mich morgens an sie erinnere. Und wenn ich mich morgens an sie erinnere, schreibe ich sie oft auf. Es kommt häufig vor, dass ich Berge rauf oder runter laufen muss und über Abgründe springen muss oder auch einen Schrank durch eine Öffnung über einer Flügeltür werfen muss. Oft treffe ich auch Menschen, mit denen ich viel zu tun habe, oder denen ich am Tag zuvor begegnet bin. Am meisten träume ich, wenn sich etwas in meinem Leben geändert hat oder ich auf Reisen bin.)

(Ich kann hier nur ein Stück aus ~~meinem~~ Traum aufschreiben (der vollständige steht aber auch in einem Notizbuch):
Also, es ist nass, es regnet oder hat geregnet und ich muss einen Berg hochlaufen. Allerdings habe ich meine Clarks Wallabees (beschämt, dass ich hier Markenschuhe erwähne) an; die Besonderheit an den Schuhen ist, dass sie eine Gummisohle haben, die auf ~~nassem~~ Grund superrutschig ist. Also, ich muss den Berg hoch und rutsche ständig wieder runter/ab. Und auf einmal kommt mir im Traum die Lösung:
Ich ziehe die Schuhe aus und laufe den Berg sicheren Schrittes – ohne Abrutschen – hoch.

Am nächsten Morgen war ich unglaublich glücklich, ein Problem in meinem Traum gelöst zu haben.)

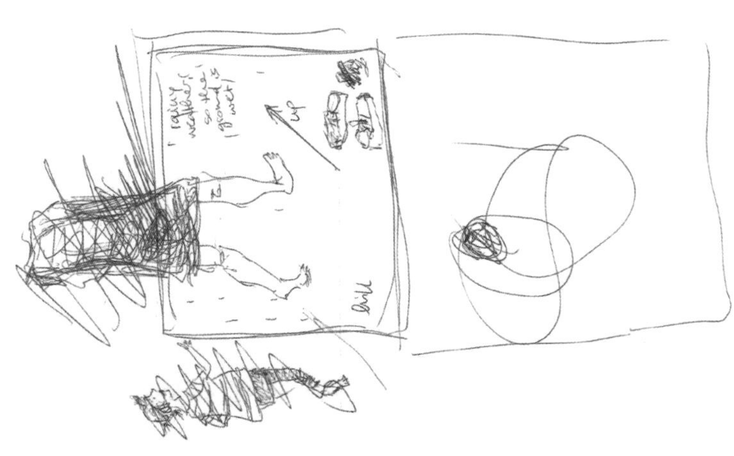

Ich bin in einer Burg. Es ist Krieg. Alle Erwachsenen sind in den Krieg gezogen. Ich bin beauftragt, die Kinder der Burg zu beschützen. Der Feind naht. Er ist ein unsterbliches, großes Monster. Er kommt in die Burg. Als er schläft schleiche ich mich an & schneide sei[n] Kopf ab, um ihn zu besiegen. Der Kopf lebt weiter. Ich reite mit dem Kopf in der Hand aus der Burg heraus, um ihn endgültig zu besiegen. Der Kopf lacht. Ich reite und reite. Ich überlege, ihn in einen See zu werfen. Ich überlege, ihn zu vergraben. Aber beides besiegt ih[n] nicht, denn er würde den Weg in die Burg zurückfinden. Schließlich finde ich die Lösung: Ich reite zu einem Goldschmied und lasse den Kopf vergolden. Dadurch wird er gebändigt, denn er kann sich dann nicht mehr bewegen.

Die Gefahr ist gebannt.

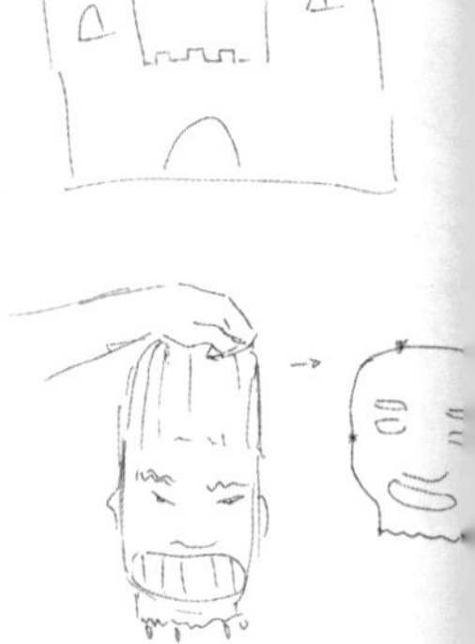

I dreamed I had a tickle in my throat, but was afraid to clear it

Viele Schienen, Straßenbahnen, die in kurzen Frequenzen hin und her fahren. Ich klettere über die Schienen, es ist recht mühsam. Unten ist ein Park, ich gehe hin, weil ich mich ausziehen muss, deswegen suche ich dort einen Busch, hinter dem ich mich verstecken kann. Aber hinter jedem dieser Büsche ist ein Obdachloser, der ein Lager aufgeschlagen hat. Plötzlich erscheint jemand neben mir der sagt: „Ja, wir haben uns hier so eingerichtet über die Jahre, es ist in Ordnung, uns geht es eigentlich ganz gut, manche haben sogar richtige Häuser." Dabei stehe ich auf das hölzerne Eingangstor zu dieser „Stadt". Etwas steht da darüber geschrieben, ich kann mich leider nicht mehr erinnern was. Ich schaue einige der Häuser an, es sind z.T. kleine Miniaturvillen, sehr luxuriös, →

nur viel kleiner, mit dorischen Säulen usw.

Ein Ehepaar zeigt mir ihre „Villa", es sieht scheinbar schick aus, aber alles ist aus Plastik und sehr billig. Wir müssen uns bücken um hinein zu gehen. Auf der blassrosafarbenen Wanne sind gelbe Zigarettenflecken.

(Blackout)

Ich versuche einem kleinen weißen Kätzchen das Laufen an der Leine beizubringen.

Draw your dream...

würde ich nur zu gern können, könnte ich dies, wäre ich wohl eine große Künstlerin.

Bevölkerte Innenstadt. Fussgänger-zone .. viele Leute .. Ich breite meine Arme aus und beginne sie langsam zu schwingen, wie Flügel. Eine Schwerelosigkeit hebt mich auf, ich schwebe, schlage kräftiger mit den Armen und entschwebe in die Höhe. Gewisse Leute gucken mir nach. Die Häuser werden immer kleiner, ich fühle mich so frei + schwerelos, fliege den Wolken entgegen .. Es ist so einfach ... Später über Wälder + Hügel, sanftes Gleiten in dem Wind ...

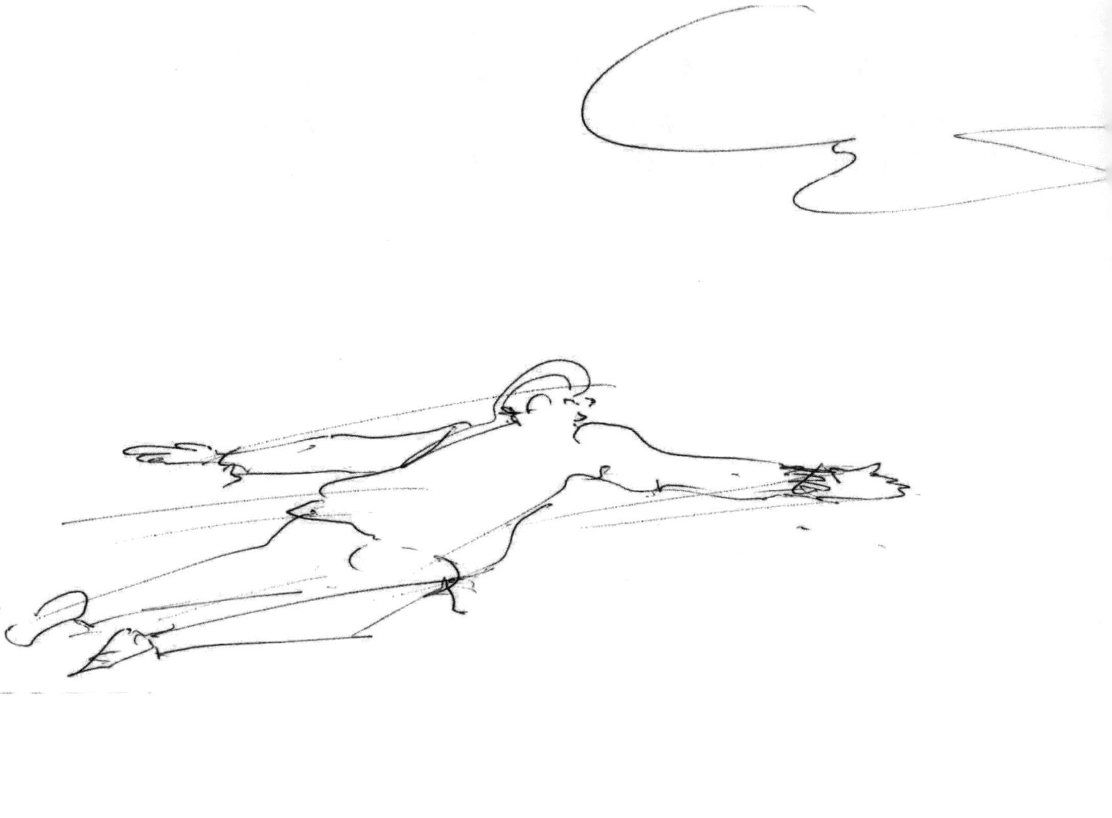

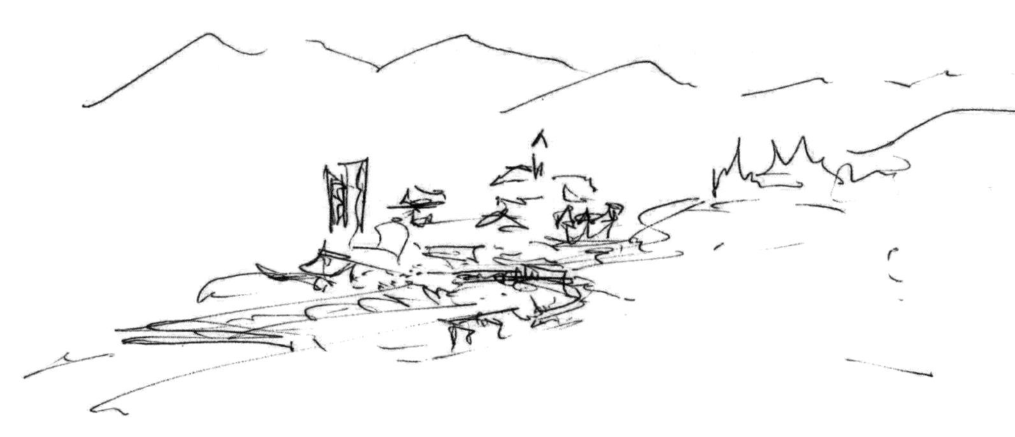

Ich war kurz bei meine
Nachbar ein 83 Jährige
Kardiopate aus Berlin
In seinen Bet lag eine
wunderschöe Junge Frau
Er war glücklich
Kenn ich auch verstehe

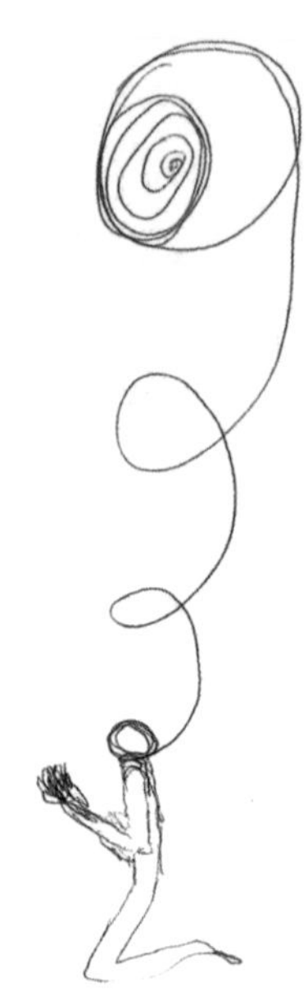

Ich gehe eine Straße
entlang (vorwärts, alleine).
Am Wegesrand liegen
beidseitig unbekannte
Leichen, deren Todesart
nicht zu erkennen ist.
Ich bin ratlos und
schaue nach anderen
noch Lebenden, aber
es sind keine zu finden.

T' ein GARTEN

ich kam zurück in d
garten meine großeltern
mit groß Bäum

GARTENPARTY
soll party sein
aber alle waren sehr
zerstreut
wie gestrandet. wie geflüchte

Es gab einen Hasen. ABER
NICHT weiß. MIT FURCHTBAREN
DARMPROBLEMEN, ER HAT
GEKOTZT. wie ~~VIELEICHT HAB ICH~~
~~MIR DAS AUSGEDACHT.~~
~~Nein! hab ich nicht~~
he wrote this best out

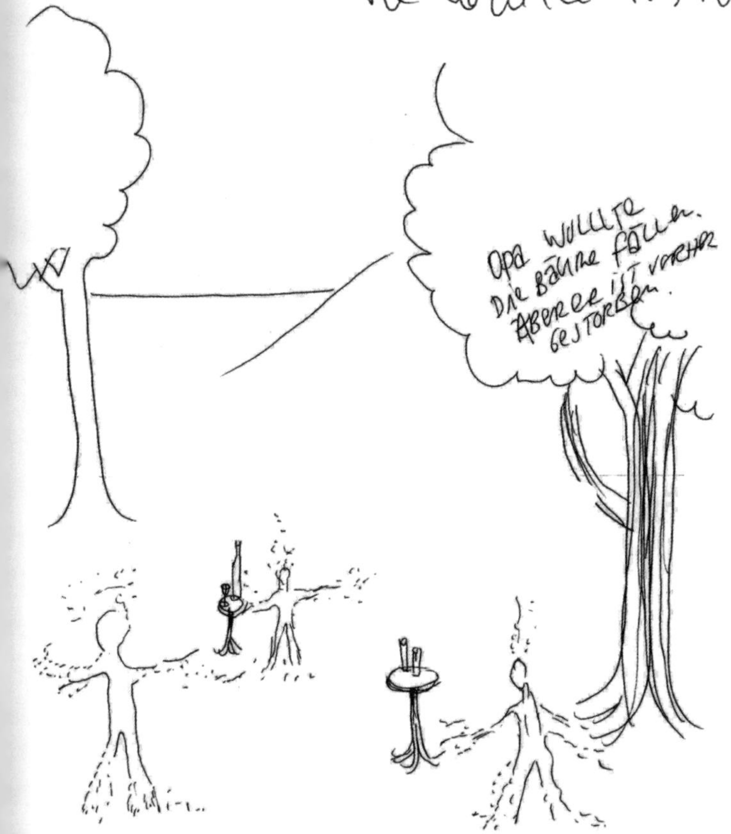

I (day) dreamt that I could do this. That I have potential and can continue on. I (day) dreamt the curtains were my friends. The outside trees danced with my eyes.

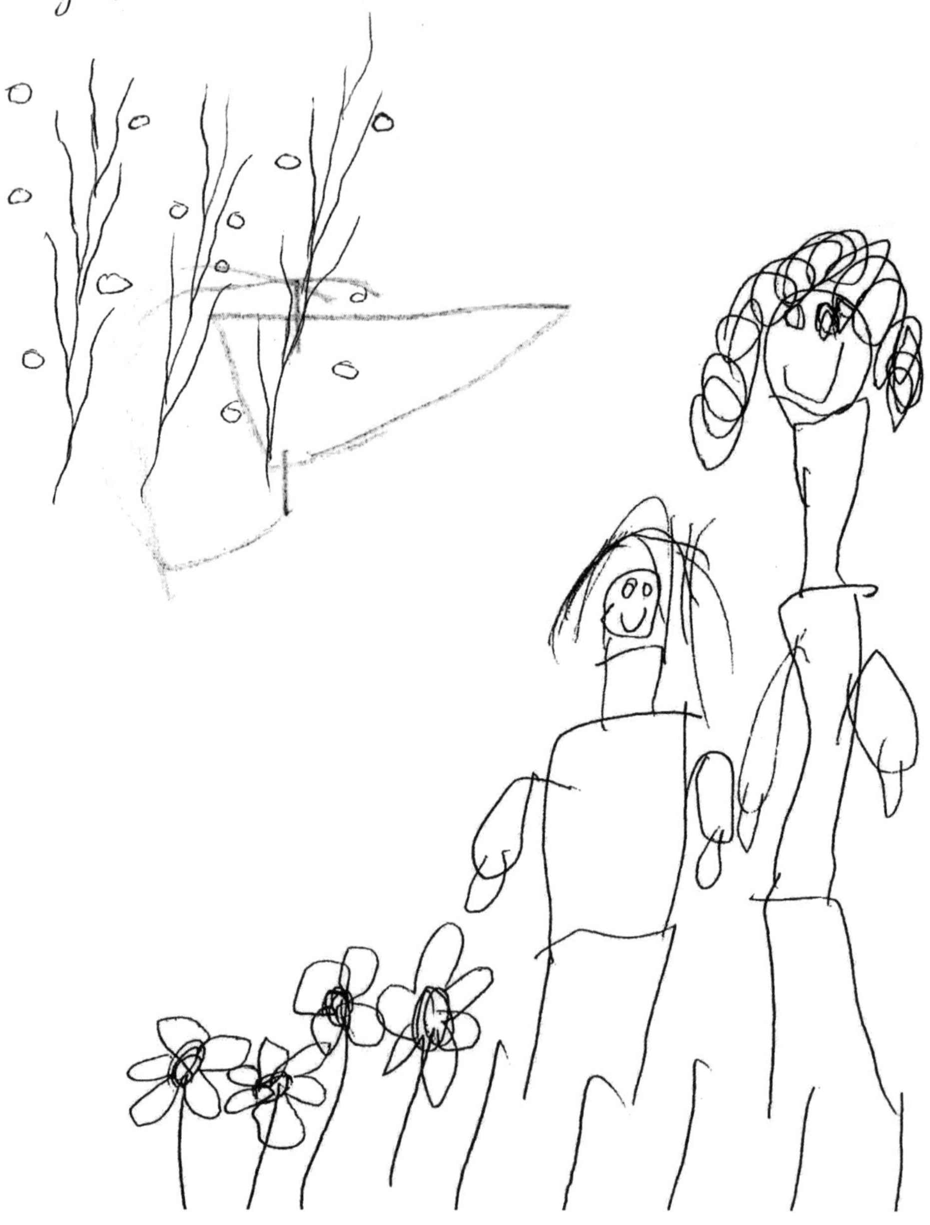

I dreamt I was hanging out with the Queen of England. But we were personally associated - I'm not sure if I was her assistant or a family member. She was certainly more fragile and withdrawn than I would have expected. At one point, for a reason I cannot recall, she was naked, and pulled me by the hand out the front door into the street, laughing.

I've been thinking a lot about my Grandma recently who is a similar age to the queen... I wonder if my dream was more about her.

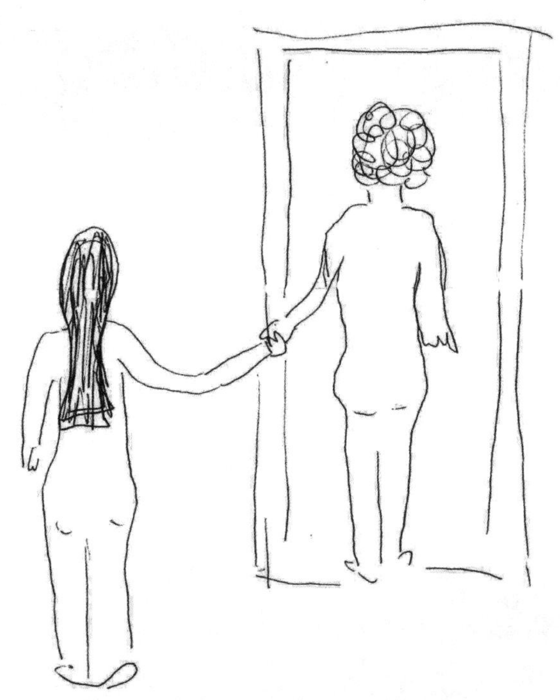

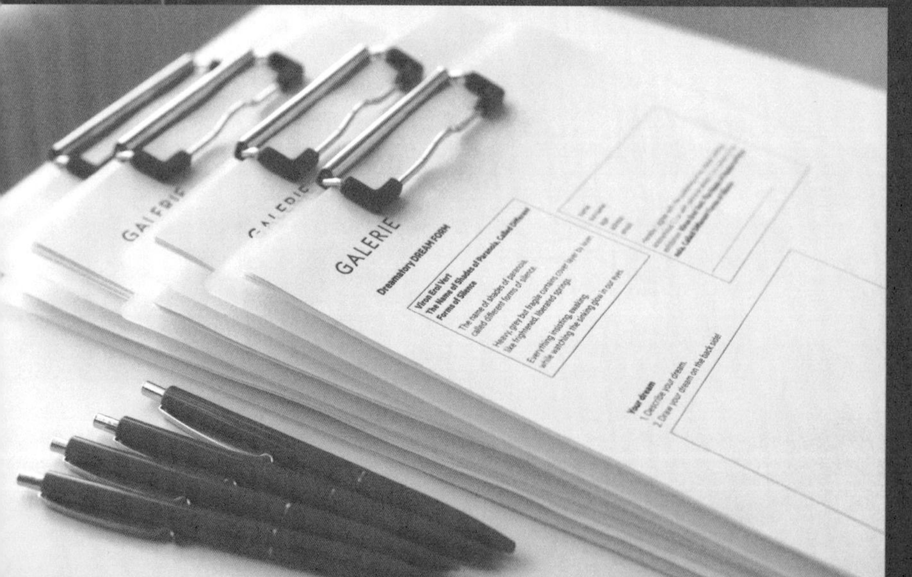
GALERIE
Dreamatory DREAM FORM
Viron Erol Vert
The Name of Shades of Paranoia, Called Different
Forms of Silence
The name of shades of paranoia,
called different forms of silence.
Heavy, grey but fragile curtains cover layer by layer
like frightened, liberated springs.
Everything imploding, awaking
while watching the sinking glow in our eyes.
Your dream
1. Describe your dream.
2. Draw your dream on the back side!

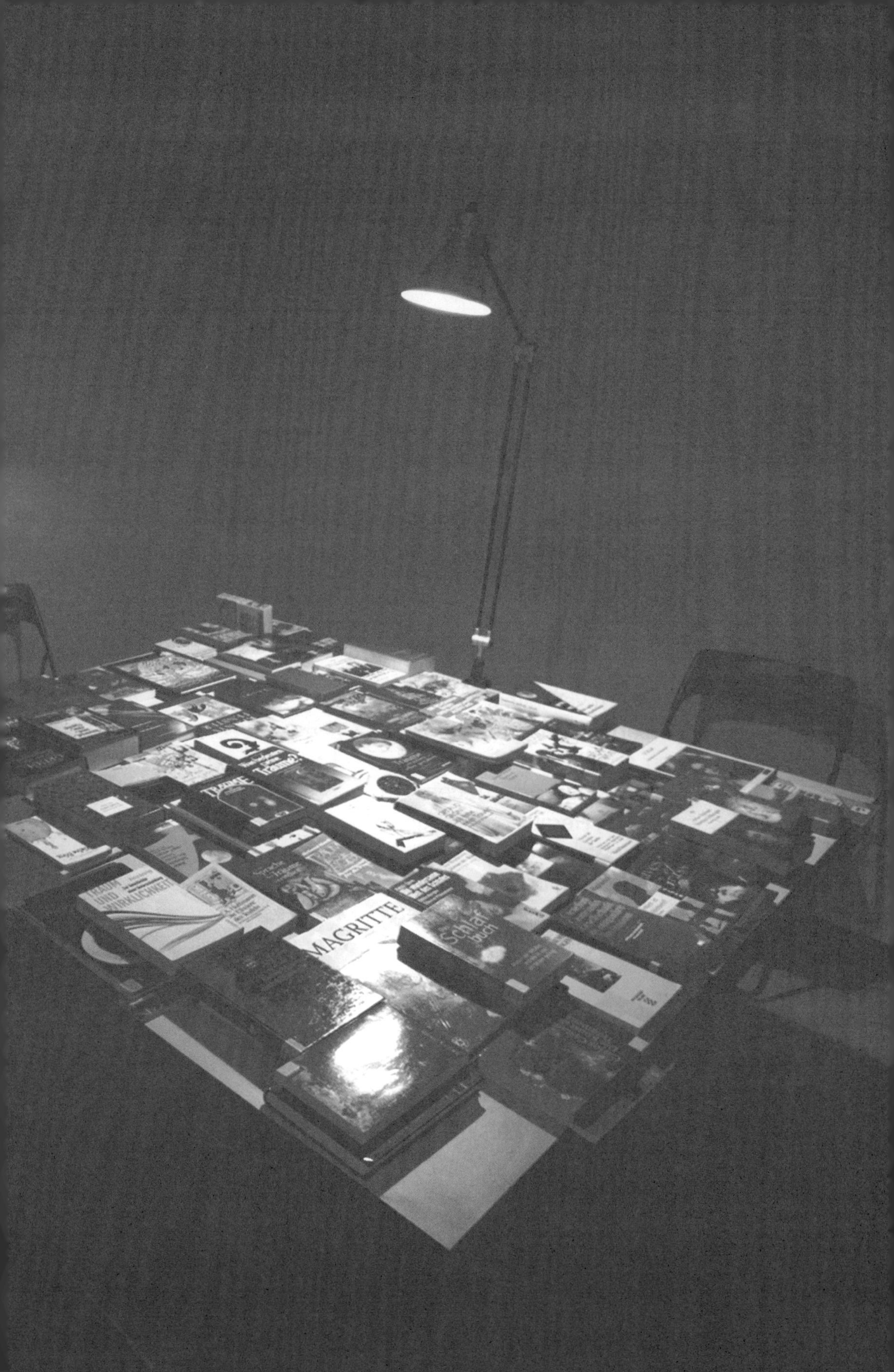
TRAUM UND WIRKLICHKEIT
MAGRITTE
Schlaf buch

Clemens Roesch

NACHWORT

AFTERWORD

DE

Das Ausstellungsprojekt »The Name of Shades of Paranoia, Called Different Forms of Silence« bezog seinen Titel von einem Gedicht, in dem Fragestellungen anklingen, die unser Bewusstsein und Unterbewusstsein zu Themen wie Identität, Zugehörigkeit und dem Verhältnis zu andersartigen Kulturen befragen, sobald wir mit aktuellen Umwälzungen und gegenwärtigen Herausforderungen wie Globalisierung, Gentrifizierung, religiösen, sozialen und politischen Spannungen konfrontiert werden.

Die konzeptuellen Überlegungen waren von dem Anliegen getragen, über die Ausstellungssituation eine Neu-Verbindung zu unseren inneren Welten, zu unseren Träumen und Ängsten zu ermöglichen. Dahinter verbarg sich die Überzeugung, dass eine Bezugnahme zu diesen tieferen

EN

The exhibition project »The Name of Shades of Paranoia, Called Different Forms of Silence« sourced its title from a poem, which asks questions about how our conscious and subconscious reacts regarding identity, belonging, and our relationship to cultures other than our own when faced with contemporary challenges such as globalisation, gentrification, religious and socio-political tension.

The conceptual deliberations were carried by the desire to establish a new connection to our inner worlds and our dreams over the exhibition's arrangement. This was fuelled by the conviction that by establishing a relation to our inner self and through tapping into our dreams and fantasies we could analyse current events from a different perspective and thereby dissolve rusty mindsets and

geistigen Schichten und ein Rückgriff auf Phantasie und Träume dabei helfen können, Vorkommnisse unserer Zeit aus einem anderen Blickwinkel zu analysieren und dadurch veraltete Denkweisen und statische Strukturen zu lösen.

In Anlehnung an Techniken und künstlerische Verfahren des Surrealismus, in denen Träume als zentrale Inspirationsquelle dienen und die Mechanismen der Ratio außer Kraft gesetzt werden und der Blick auf das Innenleben des Menschen gelenkt wird, sollte im »Dreamatory« die Möglichkeit geschaffen werden, unsere unbewussten und rätselhaften Welten aufzudecken. Durch die Schaffung eines Raumes, in dem diese Welten beschaut und über sie reflektiert werden kann, sollte ein Weg eröffnet werden, über den eigene, ungeahnte Antworten gefunden werden können. Das zentrale Anliegen bestand somit darin, die Sinne der Teilnehmer*innen und Besucher*innen für die Wahrnehmung ihrer unbewussten Regungen, ihrer Träume und ebenso ihrer Tagträumereien zu schärfen, und ihnen einen von Ruhe geprägten Rahmen zur Verfügung zu stellen, in dem man diesen Träumen

static structures.

Based on the techniques and artistic methods of surrealism – in which dreams serve as the central source of inspiration, and rational mechanisms are disabled, placing the focus on the inner self – the »Dreamatory« should enable us to reveal our subconscious and mysterious worlds.

The intention of creating a space in which this could be reflected upon was to establish a way by which individual unknown answers could be found. The main intention was to sharpen the senses of the participants for their subconscious movements of their dreams and daydreams and to supply them with a peaceful setting in which they are not faced with disinterest and suppression but curiosity and appreciation.

Through this sensibility, a consciousness for the utopian and de-escalating potential of these elements was to be created. The central urban position of this space, coupled with transparency to the inside of the gallery, was to create a fluidity between areas of reality and dream, suggesting a new sense of permeability. From the very beginning, the

nicht mit Achtlosigkeit und Verdrängung, sondern mit Neugier und Wertschätzung begegnet.

Über diese Sensibilität sollte ein Bewusstsein für das utopische und konfliktlösende Potential dieser Elemente entstehen. Über die zentrale städtische Position eines solchen Ortes, die durch die Lage der Galerie Wedding gepaart mit ihrer Einsehbarkeit von außen gegeben war, sollten die Grenzen der Bereiche, die der Realität und dem Alltag und derer, die der Phantasie und dem Traum zugewiesen werden, zum Verschwimmen gebracht und eine neue Durchlässigkeit suggeriert werden. Von Anfang an war das »Dreamatory« aber auch als Raum des Austausches und der Kommunikation gedacht, in welchem die zutage tretenden Eindrücke, Gedanken, Traumfragmente gesammelt und geteilt werden können und über welche sich ein fruchtbarer Dialog entspinnt. Die Erweiterung dieser Art von Aufmerksamkeit und Offenheit von einer individuellen zu einer kollektiven war bestrebt anzudeuten, wie eine von solch einer Kontemplation durchzogene Annäherung auch zwischenmenschlichen

»Dreamatory« was also a space for exchange and communication, in which the surfacing impressions, thoughts and dream fragments were collected, shared and turned into a fruitful dialogue. The extension of this sort of attention and openness from the individual experience to a collective experience was to hint towards how an approximation, which is infused with such contemplation can also bestow a great deal of respect and tolerance on our interpersonal encounters.
In this regard, the focus on dreaming also resembles the attempt to latch onto something that all humans are connected with and all share and which unifies them, irrespective of their generation, social background or religion. With the ability to dream, I see the potential to bridge social juxtapositions which are driving us further and further apart from each other in these times of polarisation. Because of my multicultural background and having grown up between positions with different traditions and morals, it was often necessary for me to find a synthesis between contrasting influences. Such syntheses seem to be significant when handling social tensions, and crucial to this

Begegnungen mehr Respekt und Toleranz verleihen kann.

In dieser Hinsicht stellt die Fokussierung auf den Traum auch den Versuch dar, an etwas anzudocken, das alle Menschen miteinander teilen, sie verbindet und eint – ganz gleich, welcher Generation, sozialen Schicht oder Konfession sie angehören und aus welchem Kulturkreis sie stammen. In der Fähigkeit zu träumen, die uns allen eigen ist, sehe ich das Potenzial, eine Brücke über gesellschaftliche Gegensätze hinweg zu schlagen, die in Zeiten einer zunehmenden Polarisierung immer öfter als unüberwindbar dargestellt werden. Gerade aber aufgrund meiner multikulturellen Herkunft und dem Aufwachsen zwischen Polen mit verschiedenen kulturellen Gepflogenheiten und Moralvorstellungen war es für mich häufig unumgänglich, Synthesen zwischen kontrastierenden Einflüssen zu finden. Solche Synthesen scheinen mir aber zentral, um den gegenwärtigen gesellschaftlichen Spannungsfeldern zu begegnen, und entscheidend dafür ist die Anerkennung und Betonung essentieller Gemeinsamkeiten.

is emphasising and acknowledging essential shared commonalities.

The fruitful collision of opposing elements in the »Dreamatory« should not only be limited to social questions but open up a contemporary dialogue between traditions of Orient and Occident as well as between the present and centuries past. In the beginning, my considerations tended to create a situation which put antique mythologies, archaic traditions and the Greek and Turkish cultural heritage in touch with the phenomena of our contemporary information and consumption-based society. In the end, the design of the exhibition developed into a more neutral space with an atmosphere of peace and safety and invited people to find rest on the provided beds. The references to cultural, historic and current elements could be combined into a new construct with their own holistic meaning and were shifted to a public dialogue, which was an essential part of the programme. At the same time, the largest possible space was to lend itself to the imagination of of the participants, especially its mystical and hidden corners, which are often so easily overlooked

Eine fruchtbringende Kollision von entgegengesetzten Elementen sollte im »Dreamatory« aber nicht auf den gesellschaftlichen Bereich beschränkt bleiben, sondern auch einen zeitgemäßen Dialog zwischen Traditionen des Orients und des Okzidents genauso wie zwischen der Gegenwart und älteren Epochen eröffnen. Anfangs tendierten meine Überlegungen dahin, eine Ausstellungssituation zu schaffen, die antike Mythologien, archaische Traditionen und Verkörperungen insbesondere des griechischen und türkischen kulturellen Erbes mit zeitgenössischen Phänomenen der informations- und konsumorientierten Gegenwartsgesellschaft in Berührung bringt. Tatsächlich entwickelte sich die Gestaltung des Ausstellungsraumes aber dahingehend, dass dieser zwar eine Atmosphäre der Ruhe und Geborgenheit trug und auf den verteilten Betten zum Verweilen einlud, ansonsten jedoch von neutraler Zurückhaltung geprägt war. Die Bezüge, mit denen durch eine Verbindung kultureller, historischer und aktueller Elemente neue Konstrukte mit einem eigenen, ganzheitlichen Bedeutungsgehalt geschaffen werden konnten, verlagerten sich in den diskursiven Be-

under the stress and pressure to function that dictate our everyday lives.

In this way, the concept of the exhibition transformed into a dream space, of which no art objects would remain, but only fluid intellectual results that were created in the minds of the visitors themselves.

In retrospect, I am especially surprised with how much eagerness, willingness, joy and appreciation the space was adopted, and how well it all worked out with the exhibition opening up as a social meeting point in a very natural way. A lot of people were saying that this sort of space should be a permanent installation in every district of the city, which was surprising, given its simplicity. It became quite obvious that there is definitely a need for public spaces where one can sojourn, lay down, find peace and drink tea without having to perform or spend anything and without having to be part of a certain social circle.

Only after the project had finished I realised how much the whole endeavour was gaining traction and recalling a mindset that has distinguished Berlin for years but

reich des Rahmenprogramms. Gleichzeitig sollte der Vorstellungskraft der Besucher*innen und insbesondere ihren geheimnisvollen Bereichen, die in der Hektik des Alltags und unter einem allgegenwärtigen Diktat der Produktivität außer Acht gelassen werden, der größtmögliche Raum gegeben werden.

So transformierte sich das Konzept der Ausstellung hin zu einem Traumraum, von dem keine Kunstobjekte übrig bleiben würden, sondern die liquiden geistigen Ergebnisse, die in den Köpfen der Besucher*innen selbst entstünden.

Retrospektiv bin ich vor allem davon überrascht, mit welcher Bereitwilligkeit, Freude und Dankbarkeit dieser Raum angenommen wurde und wie gut es funktioniert hat, dass sich dieser auf ganz natürliche Art und Weise als sozialer Raum geöffnet hat. Einige Male bekam ich zu hören, dass es einen solchen Ort doch in jedem Bezirk geben sollte, was vielleicht gerade angesichts seiner Schlichtheit überraschen mag. Aber daran kann auch der Bedarf abgelesen werden, der offenkundig an Einrichtungen dieser Art besteht: Orte, an denen man sich

which has been diminishing lately. A mindset that was possible due to the vast availability of free space in which people had the possibility to delve into their dreams and in which you could follow your ideas without the pressure to succeed or make profit from them. Just as these free spaces are filled like unprofitable cavities, the time that is precious to get some air, order one's thoughts and draw inspiration, seems to be dwindling and being cut short. Especially in light of the fact that in today's metropoles more and more opposing positions are colliding, a city where pressure is less dominant would have the potential to provide an environment for harmonic coexistence.

The euphoria and gratitude that I felt seeing it being possible when visitors become protagonists themselves, have free passage and are able to create their own connections, has caused a revision of my role as an artist for myself. If being an artist, which by definition is strongly connected to dreams and fantasy, can have this kind of effect on people, I feel it is my duty to encourage imagination in my fellow people. It comes as a surprise to me

aufhalten kann, sich hinlegen, Ruhe finden und Tee trinken kann, ohne dafür etwas leisten oder ausgeben zu müssen und ohne dafür mit einer bestimmten gesellschaftlichen Gruppe verbunden sein zu müssen.

Erst im Nachhinein wurde mir bewusst, wie sehr das Vorhaben damit an einen Geist anknüpft, der lange Jahre Berlin ausgezeichnet hat, gegenwärtig aber im Schwinden begriffen ist. Ein Geist, der darin bestand, dass ein großes Maß an Freiräumen zur Verfügung stand, in denen die Möglichkeit gegeben war, unbehelligt den eigenen Träumen nachzuhängen, und in denen man versuchen konnte, diese frei vom Zwang, dass etwas gelingen oder Profit nach sich ziehen muss, zu verwirklichen. So wie aber offensichtlich ist, dass die urbanen Freiräume wie unerwünschte Lücken gestopft werden, scheint auch der zeitliche Raum zu schwinden, der notwendig ist, um Luft zu holen, die eigenen Gedanken zu ordnen oder neue Inspiration zu schöpfen. Gerade in Anbetracht der Tatsache, dass in den heutigen Metropolen immer mehr Verschiedenartiges aufeinander trifft, läge auch in diesen Bereichen einer Stadt, in denen

that one can achieve this simply by creating a space in which people can be in touch with themselves and with each other, where they can explore their possibilities and find inspiration. Maybe this seems like a very obvious purpose of art, but amidst the noise of the art market, sales, numbers and trends, this simple ambition is at risk of being pushed into the background. If we think of the definition of the word museum deriving from a temple of muses, we will find that the aspiration for these spaces to be places of inspiration and communal manifestation has a deeper significance.

The diversity of the supporting programme, as well as the collected dreams and thoughts of the daily visitors, illustrated to me how one can approach this subject in so many ways and the number of people who are fascinated by it. Furthermore, I feel very encouraged to follow up on the questions that were raised during the project and turn them into artistic discourse. Especially in current times, where we have no recourse to shared myths that cover the imminent and tangible aspects of our lives, there is a justified fascination with

weniger Druck vorherrscht als anderswo, das Potenzial, sich vorurteilsfrei zu begegnen und anzunähern.

Die Euphorie und Dankbarkeit, die ich darüber spüren konnte, dass es möglich war, dass im »Dreamatory« die Zusehenden selbst zu Protagonist*innen werden, freies Geleit haben und selbst eigene Verbindungen knüpfen können, hat für mich eine Revision der Rolle des*r Künstlers*in angestoßen. Wenn diese Person von Berufs wegen stärker mit den Bereichen der Träume und der Phantasie verknüpft ist, besteht ihre Aufgabe noch viel mehr darin, diese den Mitmenschen näher zu bringen, darauf hinzuweisen und zu öffnen. Erstaunlicherweise kann das rein dadurch passieren, dass man Raum schafft und Platz gibt für die Begegnung mit sich selbst und untereinander, für das Erkunden der eigenen Möglichkeiten und der eigenen Inspiration. Zwar mag dies als eine ganz selbstverständliche Aufgabe der Kunst schlechthin gelten, aber im Getöse des Kunstmarktes, der Verkäufe, Quoten und Moden läuft dieses Anliegen in seiner Schlichtheit Gefahr, in den Hintergrund gedrängt

these imaginary worlds we all share.

Particularly in a world that has the potential to grow collectively through globalisation and the Internet, but in which heritage, passports and the documented person become more and more important again, there is a great opportunity to remember how we are all interconnected by our inner worlds, and to seize the chance to overcome the external distance between us.

And so the »Dreamatory« becomes a place to consider this community, to dream and to give these dreams the necessary space. This space can be physical or temporal, as well as a time of meditation.

This space is currently in distress and along with it the possibility to voice utopian ideas and to prepare oneself for the challenges of our time. Thus we become vulnerable to fear of the unknown which is bestowed upon us day after day. Shared dreaming can help us to free ourselves from constricting structures and pressure and ultimately from our fears.

zu werden. Wenn man sich in diesem Zusammenhang die Herkunft des Wortes Museum als ein Heiligtum der Musen vor Augen hält, vertieft sich auch ein Anspruch an solche Räumlichkeiten als Orte der Inspiration und der Gemeinschaftsstiftung.

Sowohl die Vielfältigkeit des Rahmenprogramms der Ausstellung als auch die gesammelten Träume und Gedanken der alltäglichen Besucher*innen haben mir vor Augen geführt, auf welch unterschiedliche Weise man sich dem Themenkomplex annähern kann und wie viele Menschen er beschäftigt. Darüber hat sich für mich auch die Annahme bestärkt, wie wichtig es ist, den damit verbunden Fragen nachzugehen und sich auch künstlerisch mit ihnen auseinanderzusetzen. Gerade da wir uns in unserer Zeit nicht mehr auf gemeinsame Mythen berufen können, welche die nicht unmittelbar greifbaren und erklärbaren Teile des Menschseins abdecken, besteht doch eine berechtigte Faszination für diese Welten, die wir letztlich alle miteinander teilen.

Gerade wenn in einer Welt, die durch Globalisierung und Vernetzung eigentlich mehr zusammenwachsen könnte, wieder vehementer nach Herkunft, Zugehörigkeit, nach Pässen, nach dieser Papierlichkeit des Menschen gefragt wird, liegt darin, dass wir uns daran erinnern, dass wir über große Teile unserer inneren Welten miteinander verbunden sind, eine der wenigen Chancen, die äußeren Klüfte zu überwinden.

Somit wird das »Dreamatory« zu einem Plädoyer, diese Gemeinsamkeit zu denken und zu träumen, und dafür, diesen Träumen den notwendigen Platz einzuräumen.

Dieser Platz kann räumlicher oder zeitlicher Natur sein und es kann sich auch um einen Ort des Verweilens im Inneren handeln. Dieser Platz dürfte tatsächlich gegenwärtig in Bedrängnis geraten und mit ihm die Möglichkeit, utopische Wünsche zu formieren und sich selbst auf seine*ihre Art für die Herausforderungen der Zeit zu formieren. Damit werden wir anfällig dafür, dass wir uns von allem, was man uns sonst als Bedrohung an die Wand malt, Angst einjagen lassen. Das geteilte Träumen kann uns dabei helfen, uns weniger beherrschen zu lassen von den Zwängen der Strukturen, von einem einengenden Zeitgeist und nicht zuletzt von unseren Ängsten.

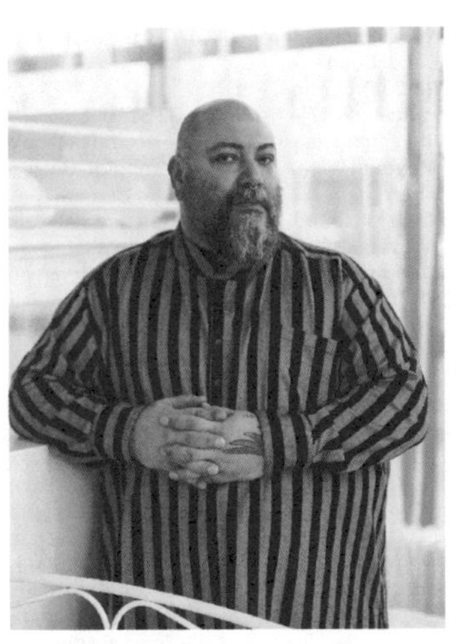

VIRON EROL VERT, geboren in Varel, Deutschland, lebt und arbeitet in Berlin, Deutschland, und Istanbul, Türkei. Seine persönliche, multikulturelle Prägung spielt eine Schlüsselrolle in der Erschaffung seiner Forschungsprozesse. Sein künstlerisches Interesse oszilliert zwischen religiösen Systemen, kultureller Identität und sprachwissenschaftlichen Erfahrungen. Vert sammelt Bilder, aufregende Geschichten und Charaktere, die ihn inspirieren, und setzt sie im Licht seiner persönlichen Vorstellungskraft, wie ein Alchemist, neu zusammen. Mit Benutzung seiner optischen Kodierungen, die er in strategischen Konzepten anwendet, lässt Vert neue Interventionen entstehen, die er wiederum verwendet, um neue Landschaften zu erschaffen. Viron Erol Vert hat einen Master in Mode Design der HTW, Berlin. Er studierte Visuelle Kunst an der der Royal Academy, Antwerpen, und absolvierte seinen Meisterschüler im Bereich Experimentelle Oberfläche an der Kunsthochschule Weißensee (KHB), Berlin. 2008 wurde er mit dem 1. Preis in der Kategorie Malerei und Illustration auf der 27th Contemporary Artists Istanbul Exhibition ausgezeichnet. 2014 erhielt Vert das Ausstellungsstipendium, verliehen durch den Kunstfond Bonn, darauf folgte das Arbeitsstipendium des Berliner Senats 2015/16. Aktuelle Ausstellungsprojekte sind unter anderem »Die Grenze«, eine Wanderausstellung initiiert durch das Goethe-Institut und den Hartware Medienkunstverein mit Ausstellungen in Moskau, Kiew, Minsk, Tiflis und Zentralasien (2016-18), »Born in the Purple« im Künstlerhaus Kreuzberg/Bethanien, Berlin (2017), welches durch den HKF und die SAHA Foundation unterstützt wurde. Weitere Ausstellungen sind »The Corundurum of Imagination« im Leopold Museum in Wien (2017) und »The Name of Shades of Paranoia, Called Different Forms of Silence« in der Galerie Wedding in Berlin (2017). Vorherige Ausstellungen waren »Where Are We Now« im NBK Berlin (2016), »Das mechanische Corps« HMKV in Dortmund und »On the moment of change there is always a new threshold of imagination« im Artspace in Auckland, NZ. Vert ist Preisträger des Villa Romana Aufenthaltsstipendiums, Florenz (2018).

DR. BONAVENTURE SOH BEJENG NDIKUNG, ist freier Kurator und Biotechnologe. Er ist Gründer und künstlerischer Leiter des Kunstraumes SAVVY Contemporary Berlin und Chefredakteur des »SAVVY Journal«, einem Magazin mit Texten über zeitgenössische afrikanische Kunst. Derzeit ist er Gastprofessor für Curatorial Studies an der Städelschule Frankfurt und seit 2015 gemeinsam mit Solvej Helweg Ovesen künstlerischer Leiter der Galerie Wedding – Raum für zeitgenössische Kunst, Berlin.
Er war als Curator-at-Large an der Documenta 14 beteiligt und ist Gastkurator der Dak'Art Biennale in Senegal 2018. Kürzlich stattgefundene kuratorische Projekte umfassen »Every Time A Ear di Soun – a documenta 14 Radio Program«, SAVVY Contemporary (2017), »The Conundrum of Imagination«, Leopold Museum Wien/Wiener Festwochen (2017), »An Age of our Own Making« in Holbæk, MCA Roskilde und Kunsthal Charlottenborg Kopenhagen (2016/17), »Unlearning the Given: Exercises in Demodernity and Decoloniality«, SAVVY Contemporary (2016), »The Incantation of the Disquieting Muse«, SAVVY Contemporary (2016).

SOLVEJ HELWEG OVESEN studierte Kunstvermittlung und Kulturwissenschaften (MA, Universität Kopenhagen, Universität Roskilde, und Humboldt-Universität zu Berlin) und nahm 2003 am Curatorial Training Program von De Appel in Amsterdam teil. Sie war kuratorische Assistentin bei BAK – basis voor actuele kunst, Utrecht, und arbeitete als Kuratorin an der Kunsthalle Fridericianum, Kuratorenwerkstatt, Kassel, bevor sie als freie Kuratorin Ausstellungen im In- und Ausland, darunter die 6. Werkleitz Biennale »Happy Believers«, Halle (2006), die 1. Kopenhagener Quadriennale »U-TURN Quadrennial for Contemporary Art« (2008), das 4. Fotofestival in Mannheim, Heidelberg und Ludwigshafen »The Eye is a Lonely Hunter« (2011) sowie u. a. die Gruppenausstellungen »Die Welt als Bühne« im Neuen Berliner Kunstverein (2009/10), »Never odd or even« in Grimmuseum, Berlin (2011), und »Entweder/Oder« im Haus am Waldsee, Berlin (2013), kuratierte. 2016 ko-kuratierte sie das langfristige Kunstprojekt, »An Age of Our Own Making«, IMAGES 2016 Kunstfestival in Dänemark mit Bonaventure Soh Bejeng Ndikung. 2018 ist sie assoziierte Kuratorin der Riga Biennial for Contemporary Art. Sie ist darüber hinaus Gründerin und künstlerische Leiterin von »GROSSES TREFFEN« in den Nordischen Botschaften in Berlin. 2015 hat sie gemeinsam mit Bonaventure Soh Bejeng Ndikung die künstlerische Leitung der Galerie Wedding – Raum für zeitgenössische Kunst in Berlin übernommen und die Ausstellungsreihen POW (Post-Otherness-Wedding, 2015/2016) und UP (Unsustainable Privileges, 2017/18) entwickelt.

DR. UTE MÜLLER-TISCHLER studierte und promovierte an der Humboldt-Universität zu Berlin im Bereich Kunstwissenschaften und Ästhetik. Sie leitet die Galerie Wedding und den Fachbereich Kunst und Kultur in Berlin-Mitte.

DR. ELENA AGUDIO ist künstlerische Leiterin von »Association of Neuroesthetics« (AoN), einer Plattform für Neurowissenschaften und Kunst, die Projekte, interdisziplinäre Forschung und Wissensaustausch zwischen Kunst und kognitiven Wissenschaften in Kollaboration mit dem Universitätsklinikum Charité sowie der School of Mind and Brain der Humboldt-Universität zu Berlin fördert.

DR. JOERG FINGERHUT ist wissenschaftlicher Direktor des in Berlin ansässigen Instituts »Association of Neuroesthetics« (AoN_A Platform for Neuroscience and Art) und erforscht als Postdoc an der Berlin School of Mind and Brain (Humboldt-Universität zu Berlin), welche Rolle kulturelle Artefakte (wie Architektur, Film, Bilder) für bestimmte Gehirnpartien spielen.

DR. HOLGER BROHM lehrt »Kulturen des Traumes« im Fachbereich der Kulturwissenschaftlichen Ästhetik am Institut für Kulturwissenschaft der Humboldt-Universität zu Berlin.

DR. MED. PASCAL GROSSE ist Leiter der Neurologischen Schlafmedizin der Klinik für Neurologie mit Experimenteller Neurologie in der Universitätsklinik Charité und erforscht neben neurologischen und psychologischen Ansätzen der Schlaf- und Traumforschung auch die Geschichte und Kultur von Träumen.

AMNA GHANI ist Doktorandin im Fach Computational Neuroscience an der Charité – Universitätsmedizin Berlin und ist Mitglied des Graduiertenprogramms der Berlin School of Mind and Brain und der AG Machine Learning der Technischen Universität Berlin.

PROF. DR. MED. PETRA RITTER ist Johanna-Quandt-Professorin für Hirnstimulation am Berliner Institut für Gesundheitsforschung (BIH) und der Charité – Universitätsmedizin. Sie ist an der Entwicklung der Open-Source-Neuroinformatikplattform »The Virtual Brain« beteiligt.

YUSUF ETIMAN lebt und arbeitet als Grafikdesigner und Artdirector in Berlin und São Paulo. Neben einem siebenjährigen Filmprogramm in dem von ihm gegründeten Berliner Raum Basso hat er für verschiedene Kontexte Filmprogramme zusammengestellt.

DR. MICHAEL R. MOLLURA lebt und arbeitet als Psychotherapeut in Beverly Hills, Kalifornien. Er erforscht die heilenden Komponenten von Musik, Performances und Bildern.
In seiner Praxis sowie weltweit über Telehealth-Internetdienste bietet er traditionelle Psychotherapie, Selbstpsychologie sowie von C.G. Jung-inspirierte archetypische Psychologie mit Schwerpunkt auf Trauminterpretation an.

DRIFTMACHINE ist ein in Berlin lebendes Künstlerduo bestehend aus Andreas Gerth (Tied & Tickled Trio) und Florian Zimmer (Saroos), deren Intention es ist, im Zeitalter von präziser und klinischer Produktionssoftware, elektronischer Musik die Klangtiefe und Unvorhersagbarkeit modularer Synthese zurückzugeben.

VIRON EROL VERT, born in Varel, Germany, lives and works in Berlin, Germany and Istanbul, Turkey. His personal multicultural history plays a key role in the creation of his research process. His artistic interest oscillates between religious systems, cultural identity and linguistic experience. Vert collects pictures, exciting stories and characters which have inspired him and recomposes them in the light of his own imagination, like an alchemist. When using his optical codes, which he applies to strategic designs, Vert originates new references that he re-uses to create a new scenery. Viron Erol Vert completed his MA in Fashion Design at the HTW, Berlin. He studied Visual Arts at the Royal Academy, Antwerp and completed his Meisterschüler in Experimental Surface at the KHB, Berlin. In 2008, Vert was awarded with the 1st price in the category »Painting and Illustration« by Aksanat in Istanbul. In 2014, Vert won the scholarship of Kunstfonds in Bonn followed by the fellowship of the Berliner Senat in 2015/16. Recent and current exhibition projects include »Die Grenze«, a travelling exhibition initiated by the Goethe Institute and Hartware Medienkunstverein at venues in Moskau, Kiev, Minsk, Tbilisi and Central Asia (2016-18), »Born in the Purple«, Künstlerhaus Bethanien, Berlin-Kreuzberg (2017) which was supported by the HFK and SAHA Foundation. »The Corundurum of Imagination«, at Leopold Museum, Vienna (2017) and »The Name of Shades of Paranoia, Called Different Forms of Silence« at GW, Berlin (2017). Previous shows include, »Where Are We Now«, NBK, Berlin (2016), »Das mechanische Corps«, HMKV, Dortmund and »On the moment of change there is always a new threshold of imagination«, Artspace, Auckland, NZ. Vert is laureate of the Villa Romana Fellowship, Florence (2018).

DR. BONAVENTURE SOH BEJENG NDIKUNG, is an independent art curator and biotechnologist. He is the founder and artistic director of SAVVY Contemporary Berlin and editor-in-chief of SAVVY Journal for critical texts on contemporary African art. He is currently guest professor in curatorial studies at the Städelschule Frankfurt and since 2015, together with Solvej Helweg Ovesen, artistic director of Galerie Wedding – Raum für zeitgenössische Kunst, Berlin. He was curator-at-large for Documenta 14, and is a guest curator of the 2018 Dak'Art Biennale in Senegal. Recent curatorial projects include »Every Time A Ear di Soun – a documenta 14 Radio Program«, SAVVY Contemporary, 2017; »The Conundrum of Imagination«, Vienna Leopold Museum Wienerfestwochen, 2017; »An Age of our Own Making« in Holbæk, MCA Roskilde and Kunsthal Charlottenborg Copenhagen, 2016-17; »Unlearning the Given: Exercises in Demodernity and Decoloniality«, SAVVY Contemporary, 2016; »The Incantation of the Disquieting Muse«, SAVVY Contemporary, 2016.

SOLVEJ HELWEG OVESEN is a curator and cultural studies theoretician (MA, Kopenhagen University, Roskilde University, and Humboldt University of Berlin) and completed the De Appel Curatorial Training Program in Amsterdam. She has curated numerous exhibitions internationally including the 6th Werkleitz Biennial, »Happy Believers«, Halle (2006), the first Copenhagen Quadrennial: »U-TURN Quadrennial for Contemporary Art«, Denmark (2008), 4. Fotofestival Mannheim, Heidelberg, Ludwigshafen, »The Eye is a Lonely Hunnter«, 2011, and the group exhibitions »Die Welt als Bühne« at the Neuer Berliner Kunstverein, Berlin (2009–10), »Never odd or even« at Grimmuseum, Berlin (2011) and »Either/Or« at Haus am Waldsee, Berlin 2013. In 2016 she co-curated the long term exhibition project, »An Age of Our Own Making«, IMAGES 2016 art festival, DK, with Bonaventure Soh Bejeng Ndikung. In 2017 she was the curator in chief of »Songs of a Melting Iceberg«, as part of the performance festival Nordwind. In 2018 she is associate curator of the Riga Biennial for Contemporary Art. Since 2015 she is artistic director of Galerie Wedding together with Ndikung, where she developed the exhibition program POW (Post-Otherness-Wedding, 2015/16) und UP (Unsustainable Privileges, 2017/18).

DR. UTE MÜLLER-TISCHLER graduated in art studies and aesthetics at Humboldt University, Berlin. She is heads of Galerie Wedding and the Art and Culture department of the council of Berlin-Mitte.

DR. ELENA AGUDIO is artistic director of the »Association of Neuroesthetics« (AoN), a platform for Neuroscience and Art, promoting projects, interdisciplinary research and knowledge exchange between art and cognitive sciences, in collaboration with the Medical University of Charité and The School of Mind and Brain of the Humboldt University.

DR. JOERG FINGERHUT is scientific director of the Berlin based »Association of Neuroesthetics« (AoN), a platform for neuroscience and art. He is postdoctoral researcher at the Berlin School of Mind & Brain (Humboldt-Universität zu Berlin) where he works on the role that cultural artifacts (like architecture, film, pictures) play for the kinds of minds we have on our evaluation of art and the role the emotion of wonder plays therein.

DR. HOLGER BROHM teaches »Kulturen des Traumes« at the department of Cultural Science Aesthetics, Institute for Cultural Science, Humboldt-Universität zu Berlin.

DR. MED. PASCAL GROSSE is head of Neurologische Schlafmedizin (Neurological Sleep Medicine) of the Clinic for Experimental Medicine, Medical University of Charité and has explored both the neural underpinnings and psychology of sleep and dreaming as well as the history and culture of dreams.

AMNA GHANI is a PhD student in Computational Neuroscience at the Charité University Hospital, Berlin and is a member of the doctoral programme of Berlin School of Mind and Brain and Machine Learning group, Technische Universität Berlin.

PROF. DR. MED. PETRA RITTER is a Johanna Quandt Professor for brain stimulation at Institute of Health (BIH) and Charité - Universitätsmedizin Berlin. She is part of the team that creates the open-source neuroinformatics platform »The Virtual Brain«.

YUSUF ETIMAN lives and works as a graphic designer and art director in Berlin and São Paulo. Apart from his seven years film programme in the Berlin project space basso which he founded, he curated film programmes for many different contexts.

DR. MICHAEL R. MOLLURA is psychotherapist and lives and works in Beverly Hills, California. He studies components of music, performance and images. In his office in Beverly Hills, California – and through teleheath Internet services – Dr. Mollura offers traditional psychotherapy, self psychology as well as Jungian-inspired archetypal psychology with a focus on dream interpretation using creative expression.

DRIFTMACHINE – a Berlin-based artist duo is comprised of Andreas Gerth (Tied & Tickled Trio) and Florian Zimmer (Saroos). They want to give back to electronic music the depth of sound and unpredictability of modular synthesis; the two factors that they believe to be increasingly lost in these times of ever more precise and clinical production software.

IMPRESSUM/IMPRINT

Diese Publikation erscheint anlässlich der Ausstellung »Viron Erol Vert. The Name of Shades of Paranoia, Called Different Forms of Silence« im Rahmen des Programms UP (Unsustainable Privileges) kuratiert von Dr. Bonaventure Soh Bejeng Ndikung und Solvej Helweg Ovesen 10.02.–08.04.2017

This catalogue is published on the occasion of the exhibition »Viron Erol Vert. The Name of Shades of Paranoia, Called Different Forms of Silence« within the frame oft the programme UP (Unsustainable Privileges) curated by Dr. Bonaventure Soh Bejeng Ndikung and Solvej Helweg Ovesen 10.02.–08.04.2017

Galerie Wedding – Raum für zeitgenössische Kunst
Müllerstraße 146-147
13353 Berlin

Herausgegeben vom/Edited by Fachbereich Kunst und Kultur, Galerie Wedding – Raum für zeitgenössische Kunst, Leiterin Dr. Ute Müller-Tischler, Bezirksamt Mitte von Berlin, Abteilung Weiterbildung, Kultur, Umwelt, Straßen und Grünflächen, Bezirksstadträtin Sabine Weißler

Ausstellung/Exhibition
Konzept/Concept:
Viron Erol Vert
Kurator*innen/Curators:
Dr. Bonaventure Soh Bejeng Ndikung und/and Solvej Helweg Ovesen
Kuratorische Assistenz/Curatorial Assistance:
Nadia Pilchowski
Praktikantin/Trainee:
Lisa Xenia Ness
Technische Leitung/Head of Installation:
Kathrin Pohlmann
Ästhetische Beratung/Aesthetical Consultation:
Gigi Spelsberg
Assistenz Konzept/Concept Assistance: Ali El Ali, Paul Springfeld

Katalog/Catalogue
Herausgeber/Editor:
Dr. Ute Müller-Tischler
Konzept/Concept:
Viron Erol Vert

Redaktion/Editorial Team:
Nadia Pilchowski, Marie-Christin Lender
Autoren/Authors:
Dr. Bonaventure Soh Bejeng Ndikung, Dr. Ute Müller-Tischler, Clemens Roesch, Dr. Holger Brohm, Dr. Joerg Fingerhut, Amna Ghani, Dr. med. Pascal Grosse, Dr. Elena Agudio, Yusuf Etiman

Korrektorat/Proofreading:
DISTANZ Verlag
Lektorat/Copy Editing:
Viola van Beek, Luise Giggel, (Deutsch/German), Mike Kitcher (Englisch/English)
Übersetzung/Translation:
Kenkelico Collective, Mike Kitcher, Michael Wetzel

Gestaltung/Design:
Form und Konzept
www.formundkonzept.de

Fotografie/Photography:
Johannes Berger, Eric Tschernow

Druck und Bindung/Printing and Binding:
optimal media GmbH, Röbel/Müritz

Vertrieb/Distribution:
edel Germany GmbH
www.edel.com
distanz@edel.com

Erschienen im/Published by:
DISTANZ Verlag

ISBN 978-3-95476-239-2
Printed in Germany

Mit freundlicher Unterstützung der Senatsverwaltung für Kultur und Europa, der Spartenübergreifenden Förderung und des Ausstellungsfonds für Kommunale Galerien/With friendly support by the Senate Department for Culture and Europe and the Exhibition Fund for Municipal Galleries

DISTANZ

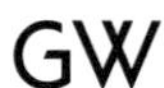

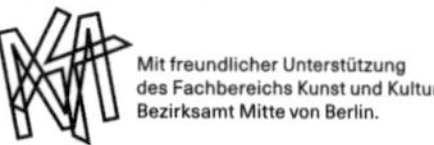